THE FIRE TOWER

Alabama Turkey Hunting

By

Bob Henderson, Jr.

ISBN: 1-4107-8929-2 (e-book)
ISBN: 1-4107-8930-6 (Paperback)
ISBN: 1-4107-8931-4 (Dust Jacket)

Library of Congress Control Number: 2003095916

This book is printed on acid free paper.

Printed in the United States of America
Bloomington, IN

Front cover photograph courtesy of MN DNR – Itasca State Park

1stBooks - rev. 09/26/03

Dedicated to my father, the senior captain of "The Henderson Team", for his relaxed patience, fatherly love, and enduring friendship.

No avid turkey hunter, who is married, can be both moderately successful at killing turkeys and have an enduring marriage without the understanding of his wife during the six week stretch from mid March through the end of April. I thank my wife, Kathy, for making both a reality in my life and also for her help with this book. Also, I thank Carolyn Rogers and Julie Coolidge for graciously devoting their time as editors.

CONTENTS

Establishing The Perspective

If you are serious about turkey hunting, and I mean truly serious, then I would like to recommend for you several pieces of literature that I feel best illuminate the true essence of a hunt with so much aura, wonder, emotion, mystique, and excitement. For those of us who set themselves apart as turkey hunters, it is these characteristics that we are absolutely infatuated with, and the authors of only a few literary works have been truly successful at bringing these characteristics to life for the rest of us to read. To progress through their pages is a near scholastic exercise entailing the study of a barbaric activity that superficially is fraught with absurdity. For who would ever expect historical literary works to capture the essence of an obsession for the death of a particular bird that is magnificent in both its creation and behavior? To those who are not true turkey hunters and do not understand, it may seem a paradoxical unity of scholasticism and barbarianism. So be it.

The vast majority of today's modern literature written on the subject at hand is too often exaggerative and only reiterative scripts of one another. They employ grandiose words for illustration and reduce my attention and interest to null. They do nothing to illuminate the aura that has so many of us gripped for life. In stark contrast, the great books of the past created imagination, rather than reiterated it, and laid a reasoned foundation of understanding for the passion of a turkey hunter. They have been successful at describing this emotion to the rest of us directly in the form of words. These great books include *The Old Pro Turkey Hunter, The Wild Turkey and Its Hunting*, and *Tenth Legion*. All three, individually, by creative communication from their authors, revealed their own little niche in turkey hunting, niches to which the rest of us can relate. Let us speak of these niches directly.

The Old Pro Turkey Hunter by Gene Nunnery is a pure story-telling book with all the enchantment of an era in the Deep South long ago. It encompasses glory and honor set around nearly mythical figures such as Gallberry Joe and The Phantom of Possum Creek. Its tales are of pure and splendid turkey hunting, lend rare insight into the weary ways of the wild turkey, and hold true to convictions against those less than honorable tactics, such as ambushing an old wise gobbler.

The Wild Turkey and Its Hunting is the oldest of the three, published in 1912, and reveals the true honor and reverence the wild turkey deserves. Edward A. McIlhenny was an authentic student of the wild turkey and crowned him, "The grandest bird of the American continent."

But without dispute, the preeminent literary work ever published about wild turkey hunting is *Tenth Legion*, written in 1970 by Tom Kelly. In actuality, it was never written to begin with, but dictated into a recorder on the way to and from the turkey woods during the 1970 turkey season. He then had the dictation transcribed and 500 copies published at the expense of his own account. One of those 500 copies found its way into the hands of some Louisiana businessmen who recognized its potential, collaborated with Kelly, and started a publishing company for the express purpose of printing and distributing this single book. The company thus born was named Spur Enterprises.

Before we discuss the content, let us review the name, *Tenth Legion*, which superficially has nothing to do with turkey hunting but everything to do with war. Titling his book with this apparent lack of connection to the subject was absolutely brilliant in propose, for the content justified its action.

Tom Kelly, who's *Tenth Legion* is articulate and descriptive, and who continues to write to this day, is simply a great writer.

The copy of the *Tenth Legion* that I have read, the one that my father owns, was published in 1974, the fourth printing of those done by Spur Enterprise. The book is hardback, the cover is tan, and below the title is a simplistic drawing of a turkey head with a sub-caption of three words written in calligraphy, "*Meleagris gallopavo silvestris.*" The importance of this species differentiation is paramount. For a book about turkey hunting, simply printing *Meleagris gallopavo* would have been appropriate, for that is the scientific name for a wild turkey, and this would seem to be a book about wild turkey hunting. But this was not a book simply about wild turkey hunting, but about the hunting of its most prominent species, the *silvestris*, or the Eastern. Tom Kelly made this distinction intentionally and abruptly.

Inside the cover, Tom Kelly gave us Southern turkey hunters a tool with which to communicate our passion to others in an intelligent and thought-provoking manner that cut straight to the very heart of turkey hunting. To read it is soul searching and self-exposing. Let us begin with Kelly's original statement found on the front inside flap (shortened in the current printing of *Tenth Legion*). It is here where he sets the stage for a concept that is so absolutely fundamental to the understanding of a turkey hunter, where he almost defines Southern turkey hunting. He does so without apology, avoiding the how to altogether, and lets us catch but a glimpse of what a turkey hunting is within his passionate point of view. He writes:

> In the South part of the United States the pursuit of turkeys is neither a past-time nor a filler for idle afternoons. It is a subculture and the members of the subculture consider it to be a serious affair and pursue their affairs with a single minded dedication and a unity of purpose that is sometimes awesome. Turkey hunting has caused more hard feelings than divorce, and it has caused some of those, too. Many people who hunt turkeys, do it with an attention to detail, a regard for strategy, tactics and operations, and a disregard of personal comfort and convenience that ranks second only to war. Like all cultists, it never occurs to them that they may be anachronisms. Supremely unconscious of the rest of the world, blind and deaf to logic and reason, they walk along their different roads in step to the music of their different drums. It is barely possible that they have a legitimate point, and this book proposes to give them the dice and let you watch them

try to roll it. And further, the book proposes to let you hear just one time and however faintly, what so many others hear with clarity and purpose all their lives, the dim and distant music of that other drum.

The stage is set, the book is open, and from there forth you will have a splendid read full of bold irony, humor, and a delicate attention to detail. If you ever from here forth read only one book about turkey hunting, devote your precious time and energy to the writings of another, whether to learn, to enjoy, or to simply understand that which has escaped you, I recommend that you turn from any consideration of reading any work other than *Tenth Legion*. If you have found disfavor with the gods and are only allowed fifty-thousand words from here forth to devote to the subject, toss this work aside and use it wiser. *Tenth Legion* is one-hundred times greater. It is a legendary original.

In January of 1997, I had the wonderful privilege of meeting my literary hero, Tom Kelly, and in the years following had the great fortune to spend enough time with him getting to know him well enough that I call him a friend. He is kind, humorous and pleasant to be in company with and speaks as if his words are falling off the very pages of *Tenth Legion* and other stories he has written since.

The writings of Tom Kelly have inspired me to set down some of my own thoughts on paper, and I will deny not that his influence shows through both my writing style and content.

In the following pages, I have attempted to provide some insight into the memories of my childhood, the true essence of turkey hunting, and of the turkey itself. I have attempted to use the English language to paint a glorious picture of the wild turkey and the pursuit of it. I have also presented some criticism pertaining to a new deviation I have seen in recent years. I have done so because I feel there is a great need for a revival of turkey hunting integrity.

The following chapters span nearly nine years of writing and comprise turkey hunting stories with a degree of opinionated argument. Each chapter opens with a short excerpt from either Tom Kelly's *Tenth Legion*, Gene Nunnery's *The Old Pro Turkey Hunter*, or Edward A. McIlhenny's *The Wild Turkey and Its Hunting*, and other excerpts appear within the body of some stories to corroborate certain facts, opinions, or arguments. The attempt is to connect the past and present and let the already printed arguments hold the water. The philosophical principles and unlegislated rules regarding turkey hunting have already been written once, and I see no reason to reword them in credit of myself. It would do all of us modern day turkey hunters a bit of good to review the thoughts of past generation turkey hunters. Besides, a few things they used to do just may have been better.

Because of the dated nature of some of my earlier stories, they may not reflect current data or laws or other facts. Additionally, I have not arranged them in chronological order as written. Instead, they are ordered according to the best flow with some requiring the information or understanding of preceding stories for best comprehension. I am of the age thirty now, which provides an unwritten credibility over any age in the twenties, and stand fervently behind each and every word I have written, including those that came from a youthful twenty-one-year-old's perspective.

So please come forth with me as we journey into the depths of Alabama wild turkey hunting. I ask you to put forth a degree of effort into the understanding of a battle within my perspective. I am not asking you to agree, but to try to understand. I hope you can laugh with me, as I intend for you to do. But I may offend some of you and your tactics of pursuit. Please do not take these criticisms personally, for I do so in an effort to bring turkey hunting back to what it should be - or at least what I think it should be. You might find that somewhere hidden deep inside your soul, you agree too.

1
THE FIRE TOWER

"He is a vain bird and craves admiration, and acts as if he were a royal prince and a genuine dude, and he will have admiration though it costs him his life. He is a gay Lothario and will covet and steal his neighbor's wives and daughters; and if his neighbors protest, will fight to the finish. He is artful, cunning, and sly, at the same time a stupendous fool. One day no art can persuade him to approach you, no matter how persuasively or persistently you call; the next day he will walk boldly up to the gun at the first call and be shot. He has no sentiment beyond a dudish and pompous admiration for himself, and he covets every hen he sees. He will stand for hours in a small sunny place, striving to attract the attention of the hens by strutting, gobbling, blowing, and whining, until he nearly starves to death. I believe he would almost rather be dead than to have a cloudy day, when he is deprived of seeing the sun shining on his glossy plumage; and if it rains, he is the most disconsolate creature on the face of the earth."

Edward A. McIlhenny, *The Wild Turkey and Its Hunting*

Little boys who do things like hunt with their fathers, often take one of two paths later in life. They either continue to do it, enjoy it greatly, or they do not, and although it is likely their fathers wish they continued to do so, they are loved no matter.

It is unknown to me exactly why these variations occur, but there are a couple of reasons one can propose. People are different, as perpendicular individualities can run within families based on a course of genetics, or altered genetics, and no one knows why. It explains relationships like high school football captains who go on to raise sons that aspire to play the trumpet or flute in the high school band. They sit in the stands, anticipate the half time, and cheer for their son, and love them, but deep inside wish it were the second half of play that they looked forward to.

Yet we are all people who are somewhat products of our environment, and sometimes the way in which we are steered while growing and learning affects our later interests and passions. Parents push us, all of us to some extent, towards certain endeavors of activities or learning because it is what they, the parents themselves, enjoy. Occasionally, the push becomes more of a shove such that a kid is forced to pursue an activity much more so for the fulfillment of the parent's desire than the kid's pleasure. It eventually reaches a point where any engagement in the activity by the child becomes a source of resentment directed towards the parent. This too, depending on the force of the push, can continue to progress until the resentment becomes so intertwined with the emotions of the activity that the outcome is a confusing sheer hatred for the activity.

It happens to all kinds of people such as sons of football stars and self-made millionaires.

Had the push not been so forceful, one may or may not have eventually enjoyed the activity. It may have even blossomed into an overpowering passion. But a push that becomes a shove will smother any possibilities of becoming a passion and turn it into a dark seed of hatred and disgust.

One of my high school football coaches was acutely aware of this possibility and strategically planned the push of his son into the sport of football by disallowing him to participate in little league football. He claimed that he did not want his son to burn out early. Whether or not his plan was a successful plan I do not know. I never liked him to begin with and never have made any sort of effort contacting him since I left.

What I do know, however, is that my father's plan was successful, and I eventually took over his push and steered my own path that veered acutely in his direction, likely even passing him, a dogleg right if you will. I love hunting, especially turkey hunting, and do not apologize for my inability to escape it.

My story begins back in 1977 at the age of four. This was the year my father first carried me into The Forest on a beautiful, crisp Spring morning.

A forest is a place where animals and trees and all of nature exist together without outside pressure from civilization. I define this distinction intentionally, because there are differences between forests and woods. Woods exist as tracts of land with growths of trees and are situated between townships and rural houses and paved roads. Within, they may or may not hold all the aesthetics and characteristics of a forest, and to some individuals, may be just as pleasurable. Woods can be of value to us hunters and may or may not hold game. But forests, conversely, are within a great expanse, always hold game, by definition, and are away from these people sort of things thus allowing one's emotions to run with the freedom and enjoyment of the isolated and pure forest primeval.

The Oak was just such a forest and was ours in the 70's and 80's.

I suppose Alabama is not all that unique in that it owns hundreds of thousands of acres of national forest land. In the northeast corner of the state, the William B. Bankhead National Forest rivals as one of the largest tracts of public land in the state. I have been there only once, and unfortunately, the visit did not in any way involve an opportunity to hunt any type of game, though I cannot deny the interest was there. The forest was full of hardwoods with scattered short leaf pines, hilly but not mountainous, and looked rich enough to hold turkeys.

The smallest of the Alabama national forests and serving the lower portion of the state, in fact adjoining the Florida border, is the Conecuh National Forest. To this place I have never been. I am sure it is a fine place to hunt turkeys.

The Oak, however, was located closer to home, in the central part of the state, and was part of the Talladega National Forest. However, that information alone will not be sufficient for anyone to determine with any reasonable confidence the place to which I am referring - even for Alabamians. For in the central portion of Alabama, there are two large tracts of national forests, each roughly 100 miles

2

apart their nearest corners. The one directly east of Birmingham, running about 100 miles in length between Sylacauga and Piedmont, is the Talladega National Forest. Southwest of Birmingham is the other tract, broken nearly equal in two halves, connected by a thin sliver around Harrisburg, and is likewise named the Talladega National Forest. Why the founding fathers of our national forests decided to take two distinctly separate forests, separated by one-quarter the width of the state of Alabama and give them the same name is a complete mystery to me.

The east section of the Talladega runs northeast to southwest and follows one of the southern most sections of the Appalachian Mountains. As such it contains some great mountains including Cheaha Mountain, the highest point in the state at 2405 feet. Although I have never done any serious hunting there, I have been there enough to be able to characterize it with some sort of accuracy. In concordance with the rest of the Appalachians, the mountains run northeast to southwest for miles at a time and are separated by valleys of half a thousand feet in vertical drop. And while I am describing the most mountainous of regions in the tract, any area you hunt will invariably involve ridges and mountains that require an element of introspection before crossing. Maybe it is for this reason and partly because I am somewhat soft inside, I do not generally think of this region of the state as holding one of the greater populations of turkeys, though I know some of the greats such as Doug Camp have succeeded in the greater part of their careers at killing turkeys there.

And while the southwestern tract of Talladega may claim the same name as its northeastern, mountainous cousin, its land was laid out distinctly different, such that I honestly cannot understand why they do in fact carry the same name, as though they are one. The half that lies south of Tuscaloosa and west of Centreville is taken up by the better part of the Oakmulgee Wildlife Management Area. The other half, south of Centreville and west of Maplesville, is geographically set apart from the management area, but its land structure is nearly identical. In contrast to their northeast cousin, both are hill country comprised of smaller ridges with no distinct pattern to their lay, such that when hunting there, none of that second guessing occurs when it comes to crossing a ridge if a turkey is heard gobbling on the other side. Additionally, whereas their northeast cousin's forest was primitive hardwood, the forest division has heavily managed their timber leaving hardwood bottoms and longleaf pine dominating the ridge tops.

This southeastern part of the western Talladega National Forest, if you can follow that, was not named anything more specific than the name given to these two separated tracts of 100-thousand-acre forests east and southwest of Birmingham. We hunted this southwest portion mostly, and as such developed our own name, The Oak. And since I hunted The Oak for so many years and at such a young age, its habitat has been permanently ingrained into my way of thinking that mixed hardwood, pine forests in hill country is about the most enjoyable land structure in which to hunt turkeys - though it is hard for me to say that I would pass up swampy bottomland along the Black Warrior River which can hold great numbers of turkeys comparatively.

So as I turned the age of four, or so my father tells me, he decided to carry me to The Oak for the first time. And carry me is exactly what he did. Though it is unlikely that I am able to remember anything specific about hunting with my father at that age, or anything at all about that first trip, I am able to recall vivid memories of joining my father during my younger years, which I define as those years less than ten years old. The ages between four and ten all run together in my mind anyway.

One of the more common recollections I have is clinging to my father's back, with my legs wrapped around his waist and my arms clutching tightly around his neck, often choking him as he carried me around piggyback. He did this in the dark, and he did this up hills as he closed the distance to gobbles echoing on the other side. He did this because at the age of four or six or even eight, I was much more than a trifle slow on foot. I moved at a snail's pace, especially if going uphill, and often got hung in briars that would literally halt my forward progress until my father carefully picked me out. Except for the moments set aside for simple lolly-gagging around, which was not that often, I for the most part was carried around the forest, which was just fine with me.

In the predawn darkness, my father would park the car alongside an old logging road that cut right off a main dirt road some ten minutes within The Oak. A few minutes were allowed for me to finish my chocolate milk and donuts while my father hid the·car keys and gathered all the needed equipment. He would then pick me up, and I would cling to his back as we scurried up a path behind us that led to the top of one of the higher elevations in the area. It was from there we listened.

Facing ahead, with the car at our left, laid a vast expanse of forest that was unbroken, hilly and full of mystery. The area was bordered on two contiguous sides by one mountainous ridge. The ridge formed a semicircle of sorts cupping the northern and eastern ends, with a shallow swag near the northern end. We stood at the northern end facing the interior, with the greater part of the semicircle to our left. Midway across the eastern side and resting atop the highest portion of the ridge was a fire tower. The car was parked at the head of the old logging road meandering from the swag down into the forest's depths. This vast expanse of unbroken land, bordered on two sides by the mountainous ridge and lorded overhead by the fire tower, we called The Canyon.

The Canyon was deep enough and wide enough to provide nearly all the territory one needed for an entire season. We hunted it hard, all of it, and it was awesome.

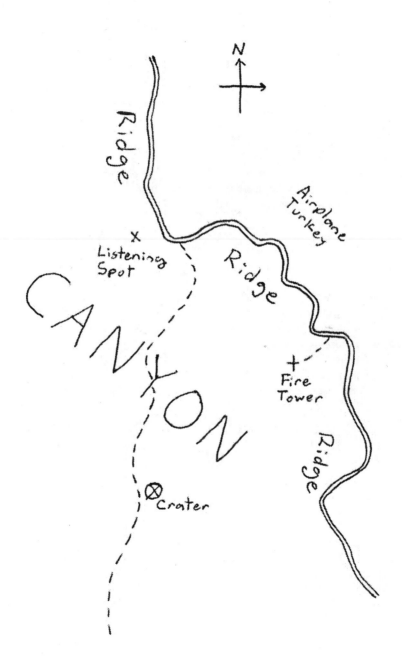

If a turkey was to gobble at the crack of dawn from anywhere within The Canyon, we would hear him and go after him. In the dark we would scurry down the side of the ridge, cross a small creak at the bottom, and begin to weave and maneuver over and around the network of hills scattered within.

Traveling like this, before the full break of sun, miles into the interior of a place called The Canyon, often resulted in a disorientation of position. But overhead stood the omnipresent fire tower, and from any ridge within The Canyon it could be seen and marked. And it was this fire tower that we could always depend on when we were lost, for it was our compass - our guide out.

Deep within this wilderness, nearly at the heart of The Canyon, laid a natural phenomenon that to a little boy was the epitome of curiosity and imagination. On top of a low ridge there was a crater of dirt, some fifty feet wide and ten feet deep. I certainly do not claim to have a great deal of knowledge of geology now, nor did I then, but even to a little boy it was blatantly obvious that the crater of dirt was exactly what it seemed—a crater from a meteorite smashing into the earth from outer space.

Nearly everyday we hunted The Canyon, we would stop off at the crater to search for turkey tracts, which we usually found, and to play and let my imagination run wild. And each time we would talk about how a meteorite had actually crashed right there, likely with a big explosion; and we would ponder if turkeys had been roosting nearby in the middle of the night, and what they thought of when it happened, and how peculiar it was that nothing grew in the crater every year.

And while visiting the enchanted crater was a pure joy, it was but a mere short rest in the morning's pursuit.

Hunting turkeys at that age was hard and lacked the excitement that a young boy requires for enthusiasm. We rarely saw turkeys and often never even heard one gobble. With exception to the moments spent playing around the crater, hunting was an attention consuming activity that I considered work over play. Thus I looked forward to the end of the morning that was allotted my time - time for me to do what I wanted. Most days, we spent my time climbing the fire tower.

Leaving The Canyon and battles to another day, my father allowed his little boy to take on an adventure that he had conquered many times before - climbing the fire tower. And being in good sport, he always followed along. Climbing the 150 feet of stairs brought me to what I thought was the height of the universe. At its top, a magnificent view of miles of treetops veined with winding dirt roads was captivating. I felt empowered as the intimidating mountains I knew from below turned into gentle rolling hills. I had transformed from a vulnerable little boy who lagged behind his father, disillusioned to the cause we were pursuing, to an omniscient eye in the sky that could see and know all below.

I must give credit to the fire tower, for its challenge and promising victory brought me back to The Oak each time with my father.

It has been nearly two decades since I last climbed the fire tower. It has been nearly two decades since I last viewed The Oak in its entirety from above, and since I have fully appreciated our true insignificance below. Oh I will do so again one day, but I will do so following behind my own son's footsteps as he climbs the tower for his first time.

My father and I occasionally visit the old public forest where we first learned turkey hunting. We park the car beside the old logging road that meandered its way into the heart of The Canyon, only now we do not get out. My father stares into the scarred landscape with few trees left standing and reflects on the moments in the sixties when he first discovered the essence of a turkey. My attention, however, is on the ever-present fire tower that watches over its land. For when I was a boy, climbing to its height and seeing for miles was Satisfaction. The labyrinth of hills and roads all became clear as we pointed out where we had ventured that morning and its relation to other areas. We were constantly stumbling into turkey rich spots, yet always searching to find more.

Today, the discovery continues. I have climbed to a new height in my awareness of the sport, mostly learning from the uncountable hours invested. If I only knew ten years ago what I know today, my beard box would be three times as large. However, if given the chance to trade in all my past mistakes for sweet success, I would hesitate for a moment and dream of the endless possibilities. Then, as I realized that these very possibilities are responsible for pulling me in the woods each Spring, I would gladly turn the opportunity down. Turkey hunting incorporates the appreciation of defeat and the dream of what could have happened. Eliminating the mistakes eliminates the true essence of wild turkey hunting.

I would like to hunt the old forest again, but it is hard to do so. It is far too crowded, for my liking anyhow, and holds fewer turkeys than most other places I now hunt. But most of these other places are not forests. They are woods.

From the fire tower, one appreciates the vastness of the forest. There is a sense of revelation as to the isolation and wildness one becomes a part of below. And it is this pure wildness of a massive forest that adds the full richness to a pursuit. A pursuit that I love. A pursuit that I could never forget.

The pursuit of wild turkeys.

2
WILD TURKEY DRINK

"To be successful in turkey hunting you must learn to rise early in the morning, ere there is a suspicion of daylight. At such a time the air is chilly, perhaps it looks like rain, and on awakening you are likely to yawn, stretch, and look at the time. Unless you possess the ardor of a sportsman, it is not pleasant to rise from a comfortable bed at this hour and go forth into the chill morning air that threatens to freeze the marrow in your bones. But it is essential that you rise before light, and if you are a born turkey hunter you will soon forget the discomforts. It has been my custom, when intending to go turkey hunting, never to hesitate a moment, but, on awakening in the morning, bound out of bed at once and dress as soon as possible. It has also been my custom to calculate the distance I am to go, so as to reach the turkey range by the time or a little before day breaks. I have frequently risen at one or two-o'clock in the morning and ridden twelve miles or more before daybreak for the chance to kill an old gobbler."

Edward A. McIlhenny, *The Wild Turkey and Its Hunting*

When I was young, on the top shelf in our den stood several objects, most not likely so different from most objects on the top shelves in other people's houses. In the middle was a small wooden box, four by six inches, stained in dark chestnut. To the left were several stacked books, none too intellectual in title, held upright by two flanked pieces of granite, and if you stood on your toes and looked close enough, you would see several layers of dust resting on top. This was after all, the top shelf. But to the right of the box sat an old half gallon-size wine jug, like those out of an old western movie, something you were not likely to see on the top shelf of another's den. It remained half full for the better part of my childhood but did not hold wine. Instead, it held Wild Turkey Drink and was only sipped upon once per year in a ritualistic fashion.

Wild Turkey Drink was sweetened hard liquor, and its ingredients were only two fold - a fifth of genuine Wild Turkey brand whisky and a box of dissolved rock candy. My father had created the concoction when I was young—in fact before I can remember.

Currently I am not much of a boozer, but I have had a sip or two (or a pint or two) of hard liquor whisky in my lifetime to know that while whisky is fiery hot with alcohol, it is already sweetened thoroughly before you do anything to it like add raw sugar. So while most of the rock candy did dissolve in the whisky, not all of it did, and a decade later, before the last sips were drunk, crystals of sugar floated on the bottom of the jug.

With the turn of each November and the fading of the Fall to Winter, my father and I would gather in the den the night before the opening of the Fall season to commence the season by taking a glass of Wild Turkey Drink together.

My father would half fill a bourbon glass for himself, and I would half fill a shot glass for myself. We would sit on the couch in front of a warm fire, talk of turkey hunting stories of old, and sip on our wild concoction.

Most of my knowledge concerning alcohol and drinking of hard liquor was obtained in my teenage years, for that is when I did most of my drinking. One particular fact I remember well is that the Wild Turkey brand of whisky is 101 proof, or just over fifty percent pure grain alcohol. Most others are only 80 or 85 proof. And what I also remember about Wild Turkey whisky is that it is 101 proof to burn the hell out of your throat if you happened to gulp a whole shot.

Not that much was different for an eight-year-old sitting with his father in his own house, in front of a cozy fire sipping on Wild Turkey Drink. It was as sweet as candy, for that was what much of it was, but if I did anything like take a sip larger than a drop or just enough to wet my lips, then I would smucker my face and cringe and gasp for air.

I never did finish more than half of my half-filled shot glass - ever.

But I drank it every November, because my father told me one very important and special characteristic it possessed. Wild Turkey Drink would make me a better turkey hunter.

Bedtime stories, cartoons, fairy tales, and other such works of literature are all created, and have the opportunity to be successful, because of one infallible fact about little children. Kids are gullible and willing to believe all kinds of outrageous and enchanting stories because they know no better. It is not their fault. Life itself, and I am not referring to the simple act of breathing and eating and crapping, is required before one is able to differentiate the real from fiction, the probable from the improbable. For life itself requires exposure to an array of events, and by repetition, one learns to differentiate these things.

I was a little kid once and was spellbound with all those stories about ginger bread houses, beanstalks, and little girls wearing red hoods.

I was gullible, so I believed Wild Turkey Drink made me a better turkey hunter.

It is this flawed character of kids that also allows them to be deceived quite easily. Santa Clause would not be so popular with the younger sect if this were not so.

Before the days I was to leave home for college, my father and I hunted primarily four areas regularly - The Oak, Clay County, Coosa County, and Betty Jean's. Back then we never spent the night anywhere near these places. We always slept at home, in Birmingham. This meant that everyday we hunted, we had to get up early and drive to the location before daybreak, and everyday we had to drive the same distance back. This could seem reasonable if the locations were near, but none of ours were. The closest location was Coosa County and was only an hour and fifteen minutes away. But it had the least amount of land of all four. Betty Jean's was an even hour and a half. Depending on the location within The Oak we were going, the trip was an hour and a half to an hour and forty-five minutes. The Canyon was an hour and thirty-five to be exact. And the farthest of the four, Clay County, was guaranteed an hour and forty-five at the least.

An hour and a quarter to an hour and three quarters is not a short distance to drive every morning before the crack of dawn. If you consider the time needed on the front end to dress and load the truck and on the rear end to walk through the woods up to a mile away under the blackness of night, then the operation becomes lengthy and requires a very early rise indeed. McIlhenny discussed rising at one or two-o'clock in the morning and riding up to twelve miles to a location before light. He later says, "Once I saw fifteen gobblers feeding in a hollow between two ridges. I dismounted from my horse, crawling to the brow of the hill in order that I might peep over and have a good look at them." I myself have risen at two-o'clock in the morning, not frequently, and once at half past one to go turkey hunting as he advises. But never have I done so to braze the chilled air on horseback as he did.

There are those who hunt turkeys, and those who are turkey hunters. There should be no confusion as to which McIlhenny was.

In my earliest years, we hunted primarily The Oak. Before I ever got excited about going turkey hunting such that dealing with that associated problem of insomnia was not an issue, my father would carry me from my bed at three in the morning to the car. In the back seat, he would lay me down on a pallet of blankets and pillows and cover me up.

Since young boys require sleep and have trouble staying awake in cars in the dark at half past three in the morning, my father drove the hour and thirty-five to The Canyon while I slept in the back seat.

Twenty minutes from the dirt road that led into The Oak, our route ventured off the main highway onto the Rabbit Road. Just as the Fire Tower often ended our days hunt, the Rabbit Road began it. My father would wake me up in the back seat as we made the turn, and I would jump in the front seat, excited, and watch with all of my attention for little wild rabbits scurrying across or alongside the road.

The Rabbit Road ran somewhere around five miles in length, and for the most part, was lined on both sides with fields and interspersed timber providing prime habitat for little wild rabbits to live. Rabbits were plentiful and invariably caught by the headlights under the dark of night, both in the road and along its grassy shoulders. Watching for them was an activity that delighted a little boy.

At the road's end, I would jump back in the back seat where my father had laid out my hunting clothes and boots on the floorboard. I would get dressed, jump back up front, and eat a six pack of white powder donuts and drink a single serving carton of chocolate milk for breakfast. It seems that I was always eating the last donut and taking my last sip of milk as we pulled up to The Canyon. It was like clockwork!

The date for Easter Sunday is officially defined as the Sunday following the Paschal Full Moon date for the year and is overly complicated to calculate. It is supposed to retain the same season and same relation to the full moon as the date Jesus arose from the dead in 30 A.D. The calculation involves several tables and multiplications and additions of a whole array of nonsensical algorithms. How to do it I do not know, nor do I care, for the dates are already calculated for each year in the next few centuries. What I do know and care about is that Easter Sunday always falls within Alabama's Spring turkey season. It has done so my whole life.

Alabama's Spring turkey season currently runs from March 20th to April 30th in most parts of the state. Several counties end it April 25th, as they also have a Fall season. During my lifetime, the earliest Easter date occurred the year I was born on March 26th, and the latest occurred just last year on April 23rd. If I am fortunate enough to live to the ripe old age of 100, or the year 2073, then the earliest date of Easter I will personally witness, will be March 25th, which will actually occur twice, and the latest will be April 24th, both just inside Alabama's season with comfortable margins. Providing that the Alabama Game and Fish Department does not decide to change the season's dates in the future, which I say is 50/50, I can continue to associate Easter Sunday with turkey season.

Easter Sunday was the most special day my father and I hunted together. We went every year, got up at three a.m., drove to The Oak in my early years, Betty Jeanne's or Clay or Coosa counties in the later years, hunted, and returned home in time to dress and be at church by ten-thirty. If Easter occurred before the daylight savings break, we hunted from five-thirty to eight-o'clock, drove the hour and fifteen to three quarters minutes back home, depending on where we hunted, and had ample time from nine-thirty to ten-thirty to shower, dress, and make it to church. If Easter occurred later in April, after the break, we stretched the hunt from six-thirty to eight-fifteen, high tailed it home, showered and dressed and just barely made it in the church doors before the end of the first hymn.

For some puzzling reason, my father has always held the superstition that the date of Easter Sunday directly affects the behavior of turkeys in regards to the dates of their peak gobbling. As if turkeys have some instinctive knowledge of the Paschal Full Moon date, he feels that early gobbling seasons run in concordance with early Easter Sundays, and late gobbling seasons run in concordance with late Easter Sundays. I have witnessed seasons that opened with the leaves half out and where my father spent the first two weeks working turkeys every day, even killing one or two, and then on the first day of the third week, should it be windy and cloudy and he hear he nothing, and should Easter fall in the latter part of April for that year, he will proclaim with a straight face that the turkeys are simply not gobbling well yet. It makes no difference if he hears ten turkeys gobbling their heads off on March 20th, he will believe that gobbling will not really get going until later in April if that is when the Paschal Full Moon falls. It is an astonishing display of illogic and superstition.

But what he did know about Easter Sunday, and was correct about, was that the holiday provided him with an opportunity to make one day we hunted together far more special and enchanting than usual.

At five a.m., we would turn on the Rabbit Road, my father would wake me up, and I would jump in the front seat and watch with every little bit of my attention for rabbits crossing the road - wild rabbits and Easter Bunny rabbits. The Easter Bunny was there, somewhere to be found, on the Rabbit Road every Easter morning, though I never saw him, but my father did. It just so happened that I was never looking at the right side of the road he was on when we passed him. My father always saw him, always pointed him out, and I was always a tad too slow to catch him with my own two eyes. I never did see him once.

I would then get dressed, eat my donuts and drink my chocolate milk, and we would get out of the car and hunt The Canyon as if it were any other morning -as if it was ordinary, but it never was.

At some point during the two and one-half-hour or one-hour and forty-five-minute exercise, depending on which side of the daylight savings we were on, my father would stop the car and have me step out and yelp down a hollow; or he would have me walk 100 yards down this or that path and yelp; or he would lead me out of the woods across a certain ridge. Funny what I always found.

In *The Good the Bad and the Ugly*, Tuco never knew in which grave the money was stashed. He only knew the name of the cemetery. Without Blonde, he never would have figured the stone with nothing written on it represented the grave marked "UNKNOWN." It is a good thing Blonde was not shot.

Tuco would have been empty handed without Blonde, just as I would have been empty handed on Easter morning without my father. For every Easter morning that I missed seeing the Easter Bunny hopping along Rabbit Road, the Easter Bunny always found me in the woods. Down in the hollow my father would have me yelp, or beside each path he would have me walk, or on top of that certain ridge he would lead us out by, I always found an Easter basket hanging on a limb.

Those tales by Mother Goose and characters like the Tooth Fairy and Easter Bunny carry no credibility with this twenty-eight-year-old.

Wild Turkey Drink does.

I am married now and starting to ponder those future things that all married adults are supposed to do. One day I will have my own son to deceive and mesmerize with enchanting stories and tales. One day, I will go forth from a candy store and head to the nearest liquor store, preferably in that order, and buy one item from each - one for little children, and one for grown men. I will mix them in an old western wine jug, place it on the top shelf in our den, and sit as a father with my son in front of a warm fire on a cold November afternoon. We will take in a little bit of that burning sweet knowledge together.

We will sip on some Wild Turkey Drink.

3

THE BLOOMING

"It is a lovely time of the year. There is as yet not much color to the woods but there are some early hints and stirrings, mostly muted pastels or pale chalks with only two or three brights for contrast. The shrub form of buckeye is in full leaf and flower, and the red maple is in fruit. Both the buckeye flower and the maple seed are a bright red—a gaudy, primitive, barbaric red. Blackberry, sweetgum, and huckleberry will be in the beginning of early leaf in the understory, and witch hazel, tag alder and river birch in the middle story with both stories in pale, pale greens. All the oaks are in catkins, the long fuzzy strings that come before the leaf, and make a background of pale buff and brown. Dogwood shows occasional streaks of sharp white, and in the river swamps the yellow top makes splashes of chromium yellow."

Tom Kelly, *Tenth Legion*

Tom Kelly once wrote of the sequential changes relating to the closing dates of Spring turkey season that occurred during the Twentieth Century as legislated by the state of Alabama. It was originally less than a month long and despite all its changes, has always opened as it does now on March 20th, the first official day of Spring. Originally, however, it used to close a meager three and a half weeks later on April 15th. In time, the season was extended to April 20th, then the 25th, until finally all but a few counties axed the Fall season and extended it yet again to April 30th, nearly doubling the original three and one-half-week season.

The current length of season is certainly generous, and my compulsion is so great that I hunt all the way from the beginning to the end, but I do not necessarily enjoy all of it. I am absolutely worn out, and to be quite frank, a little sick of hunting by the end - it is hot, the nats can drive you literally crazy, and the mosquitoes can just about suck you dry.

Now it seems that the great state of Alabama, which I have always held in high regards, has gone and done something foolish. Instead of extending the season on the tail end as they did in the past, they have moved the sacred opening date up five days to March 15th giving us a forty-seven day season. It is now not only possible to hunt turkeys as Winter officially begins on December 22nd, but now you can hunt them the last five days too. When this season comes around, I may finally understand a bit of Tom Kelly's frustrations way back then. The last week will surely be carried out under bitter exhaustion.

Two years ago, the state pushed back the duck season to close the last day of January. It was a good move and valiant effort, but I still do not think the ducks made it down in time to shoot them this year. Now deer hunters are calling for extended seasons themselves. With the idiotic removal of the Fall turkey season and

...e seemingly merging of the deer, duck and Spring turkey seasons, I honestly wonder if one day we will have one single season to hunt them all - a uniseason if you will?

I can tolerate just about anything the state of Alabama has a mind to do with the season as long as it never adopts the idiocracy of some states by closing Sundays to hunting. The argument that game needs one day a week to rest is blatant stupidity bordering on hypocrisy.

It used to be, or so I am told, that in the old days, turkeys never gobbled during the first week or two of season. You could go and mess around in the bitter cold and possibly kill one, but there was not going to be much of that coveted gobbling involved. It seems now that things have changed, and though the first week certainly lacks all that action seen the first week in April, I can usually find a turkey gobbling somewhere. Clay County seems to retain a bit of the old, as turkeys never gobble there before April 1st. But in Pickens County, however, I once heard eleven turkeys gobbling at the crack of dawn three days before the season even began.

Science tells us that the length of daylight that varies daily within the seasons governs the sexual cycle of turkeys. With the approach of Spring, the daylight hours lengthen, stimulating turkeys' pituitaries, thus changing their hormones. It is these hormones that induce gobblers to gobble and hens to lay eggs.

If this explanation were all there was to it, then turkeys would start gobbling on predictable dates each year. But they do not, and it has often been believed by many that more is involved. In fact, if you get to hunting turkeys often, you will begin to believe there is a far more intricate association of multiple variables that we do not even know of yet.

One old fable says that when the redbuds are blooming, the turkeys are gobbling, and this has nothing to do with opening dates set by lawmakers or the number of daylight hours in a given day. In similarity, my own personal fable holds that when the dogwood tree blooms in the state of Alabama, turkey season has begun.

The blooming of wild dogwood trees usually takes place in the latter part of March, the time God intended for it to happen. And, often, this may occur a few days, or even a week or two, after the first legal day to shoot turkeys. Now if this is the case, I am sure not going to wait for the blooms to open before I enter the woods. Turkeys gobble in disregard to the presence of dogwood blooms. I seriously doubt the increase of light in the woods reflecting off the white blooms has any added stimulatory affect on their pituitary. I have even killed a good number of early Spring turkeys before the blooms have opened. But turkey season, in accordance with my own personal definition, does not officially begin until the wild dogwoods in hardwood bottoms and pine hillsides open their blossoms.

If memory serves me correctly, it was nearly the same time I began to appreciate turkey hunting that I began to notice the dogwood tree. My father had carried me around through The Oak for a good many years before this time. We hunted The Canyon, and I can recollect walking for hours deep through unbroken tracts land.

Among those characteristics most unique to The Canyon, a few remain especially vivid in my memory. From high above, lording over the land stood the fire tower, and at the heart, down below, all the mystery and enchantment was preserved within the crater. Scattered within was an array of random hills and ridges with no purpose to their lay. Between these ridges, in the hollows, the hardwoods dominated with bamboo-lined creeks. But on top, tall, longleaf pines reined with a dusting of oaks and wild azaleas underneath.

From the limited knowledge I have of pine trees, I know there are four common species that grow in the woodlands of Alabama, or should I say in Alabama's turkey country, for who knows what grows atop the Appalachian Mountains in the northeast section of the state. I have never hunted around slash as it only occurs close to coastline. Loblolly fills most pine plantations, is a monotonously boring evergreen, and does little to stir my interest, though I am not a forester and do not judge wood by its cord value and growth rate.

The other two, short and longleaf, do stir my interest, because they grow wildly in many of the places I hunt. Shortleaf dominated Jasper County, was not grown from replanted plots, and since Jasper held turkeys, and I used to hunt Jasper, I see it as valuable.

But my favorite pine is the longleaf, for it is the most aesthetically appealing of them all, and it dominated the ridge tops within The Canyon (which is a rarity I am told, as longleaf stands usually only occur along the coast, like slash, and require virtual elimination of every life form but itself on the area it occupies to be regenerated). Just as the aimlessness pattern within The Canyon was forever ingrained into my way of thinking that mixed hardwood and pine forests in hill country is about the most enjoyable land structure to hunt turkeys in, old longleaf pines fulfill the emotion that old longleaf stands are the most enjoyable pines to hunt turkeys around, if you have to have pines to begin with. Pines will not grow in swamp bottomland, thank God.

But more than simple and pure aesthetics, longleaf is indisputably the most comfortable tree to sit against, and as such, we sat next to a whole lot of them in The Canyon. Longleaf pines are so lush with long needles that they pile up into thick layers on the ground from years of shedding. Consequently, a remarkably soft bed of straw to sit or nap and relax can often be found at its base. With a minor degree of remodeling, this bed can be shaped and molded into an unparalleled seat of comfort. You could sit for hours if you pleased.

But within these vast tracts of hardwood and pine grew a different kind of tree that held a uniqueness of character all its own. This tree was much smaller, appeared more fragile, and did not compete with the other trees for canopy space overhead. It took a different approach. It quietly grew underneath in the shade, rarely approaching half the height of those old longleaf pines, but displayed itself with subdued brilliance, particularly in the Spring.

As I said, the dogwood is a small tree. Its base rarely exceeds that of eight inches, and for this reason, is in actuality of no utility to a turkey hunter. Sit at one, and it will no more break your outline than six-year-old loblolly pine. Besides, its bark is so rough surfaced and full of knots that your back will throw fits at you for sitting up against one.

I like dogwoods because they add splendor to the woods. Not only are they beautiful when in bloom, but also their branching patterns possess a unique element of architecture.

Each branch comes off the trunk, and rather than filling out the entire space it has to work with, seems to reach out in sheets, or two-dimensional horizontal planes. Each successive branch does so in a similar manner only rotated about the tree a little and on a different plane of elevation. Furthermore, the tree is careful enough to limit its number of branches not crowding these sheets from above or below.

Go observe this for yourself, and you will see what I describe. But take note - dogwoods that grow in the open do not adhere to these rules. The excess of light seems to disrupt this pattern of growth, and they get over stimulated and do too much branching. They can look as if they are tall bushes. Only the dogwoods that grow under a full canopy display this architectural characteristic - under canopies like the ones at in The Oak for instance.

While the architecture of the dogwood is inspiring, when in bloom, it is majestic. Now I will readily admit that the dogwood flower in and of itself is not as radiant as many other flowers of the flowering plants and trees. I would no sooner have substituted dogwood blooms for the roses I gave my wife when I asked her to marry me than to quit turkey hunting and take up moose hunting.

But it is not the dogwood blossom, solely, that confers splendor to the tree. Rather, it is the manner in which it is presented in the wild that makes it magnificent. Most flowering trees make the mistake of over branching and, subsequently, overcrowding their blossoms. While they may be colorful and brilliant, and I absolutely enjoy their picturesque, they are usually crammed into every square inch of space on the surface of the tree, leaving no appreciation for architecture and engineering. But since dogwoods are aesthetically engineered to begin with, when they bloom, they do so against the backdrop of well-planned scaffolding with precision and class. It can be simply beautiful.

Through the years, I have noticed different subspecies of dogwoods that grow around the state. I am not intending to define a sub-subspecies of dogwood to credit my name but have simply taken notice of variances of height and bark structure and bloom size for different dogwoods in different areas. Most of the dogwoods you see around neighborhoods, those that were bought at local nurseries tend to have blooms that measure approximately two inches in diameter. But the dogwoods back in The Forest, especially those deep in The Canyon, boasted of four or five-inch blossoms, comparable to the size of a coffee dish. They were brilliant white, and supple, and stayed in good appearance for at least a month after opening.

Couple these brilliant white blooms scattered about in a frenzy of various shades of browns and light greens as the Spring woods come to life, and what you are left with is a wonderfully artistic scene.

The progression of a turkey season is a marvelous time of transformation of the forests. Opening day is full of dull grays and browns, and your sight can be upwards of a one or 200 yards, depending on the age of the growth and the lay of the land. But slowly, all before your eyes, the woods take life and close in. With each new week, the woods become more interlaced with various shades of light greens as the tender premature leaves emerge from their branches. It is these lighter shades of green, when the leaves are only a quarter or half out, and you can still see far enough to enjoy, that I love. It is at this point in the season that the dogwoods are about a week or two into their blooming, and the woods are full of various shades of greens scattered about a back drop of grays and browns with brilliant whites grouped and spread about in the distance.

If I were given the opportunity to kill a turkey anywhere and under any circumstance I wished, I would do so back in The Canyon, 100 yards away from the crater. I would be seated against an old longleaf pine atop a ridge. It would be the end of the second week of season and the leaves would have just started coming out. My watch would read ten-thirty. There would not be a breath of wind in the air nor a cloud to be found in the deep blue sky. My turkey would gobble, ten or so times, down in a hollow, within a matter of thirty minutes. I would then have him top the ridge and step out underneath a blooming dogwood with pure white blossoms the size of your hand, and stand there at twenty-four yards, looking for that hen with every bit of attention he owns. When I say stand, I mean standing tall, with his feet together, his back high arched, his feathers sucked tight to his slim, sleek body, and that neck reaching up four feet. I would then shoot the turkey, as should be done, and have an artist sketch the whole scene on canvas to hang above my fireplace.

Now that you have a good understanding of my fascination of dogwood trees, let me say that this enjoyment can, and has had detrimental affects on my state of well being at certain times of the year. I stated before that dogwoods are intended to bloom in the latter part of March. But, as is the case with most aspects of life, they do not always fall in line and do what they ought to do.

Sometimes, as Winter approaches its end, there comes a heat wave across the state of Alabama that disrupts nature's equilibrium quite a bit. Warm spells such as this are common in February, and occur almost yearly. They get the birds to singing and chirping and even make me want to gobble a time or two on my way out the door in the mornings. But these warm spells normally give way back to Winter air, and in a few days, everything is back on track. But these heat waves can sometimes persist up to three or four weeks and get every flowering tree and plant bursting wide open, which is all good if you are looking to take a stroll in the park with your girl. But it has two destructive influences on my turkey hunting, the first being my personal enjoyment of the aesthetics of the woods and the second related to the quality of the hunting, though unsubstantiated by scientific evidence.

Regardless of how warm the days in February and early March have climbed, it is a well-known fact that the opening day of turkey season is going to be cold. It invariably happens, without fail, and is similar to the phenomenon experienced on the opening day of dove season, though the patterns of weather are reversed. Early September days may tease you with cool, pleasant afternoons, but the third weekend is always going to be blistering hot and sunny, and you cannot do anything about it but sit in it and bake.

If the dogwood opens its blooms too early, before the second half of March, it runs the risk of having to fight off the cold snaps that occur normally in March. By cold, I mean in the upper twenties or low thirties, below freezing, and the dogwood flower can withstand this extreme stress about as well as my father.

For those of you living in the states up North, I ask you not to laugh out loud at that statement too hard. Temperatures that dip below the freezing point can cause considerable commotion for Alabama turkey hunters, and I have never seen anyone hate it more than my father.

This is not the case for deer hunters, mind you, for they have the luxury of being able to bundle up with thick-layered jackets and sit cozy in a stand. But we turkey hunters are faced with a more serious dilemma. If we wear too much clothing, and that turkey gobbles a half-mile off, we are going to nearly burn up crossing ridges to get to him. Then, after sitting a while, and after that sweat begins to loose a little of its heat, the freeze begins to chill our bodies like an ice cooler. And if we wear too little clothing, well, then we just start to chill a bit sooner.

One night in the upper twenties will burn dogwood blooms. Their growth is stunted, they shrivel to a degree, and the pedals become tainted brown. It ruins their brilliance for the entire season. While this is not going to affect the number of turkeys I am going to kill the upcoming season, it will affect the aesthetics of turkey hunting that I so greatly enjoy.

The other problem is born from my personal definition of the beginning of turkey season. When I see dogwoods blooming around the streets of my neighborhood, I feel that turkeys across the state are gobbling, and I cannot go hunt one if that is March 5th. I understand that the amount of light in a day is responsible for the reproductive hormonal cycles in turkeys, but I cannot help feel that warm temperatures are largely influential too.

If the dogwoods are blooming, that means that the weather has been warm for a while. If the weather has been warm for a while, that means turkeys are gobbling. And if that occurs before the season opens, my father and I run around panicking that the turkeys are going to be finished with their business before the state lets us shoot one.

Obviously, I am embellishing this story to a degree, but I do believe turkeys start gobbling and hens start laying eggs a little sooner if the weather has been ripe - and this, in fact, does affect my turkey hunting.

At the beginning of a normal season, I have found there is a short time when gobblers are seeking hens, but the hens have not quite yet become equally interested. Gobblers in this case are alone and much desirous of a hen. This is supremely advantageous, for much of the competition is eliminated. That gobbler will be a little more willing to come to your calling. Based on past accounts, I estimate this usually lasts a week or so.

But if the turkeys start their mating season early, due to warm weather, say a week early, you may not be present to capitalize on this awesomely productive period. Instead, come opening day, you might get stampeded by fifteen hens galloping towards your gobbling turkey.

I propose two effects will occur as a result of the state of Alabama changing the opening date of season to March 15th. For those years in which the dogwoods shamefully open their bloom early, we may all benefit and catch that early advantageous disequilibria between male turkeys and female turkeys. But more often, I say, we are going to spend five extra days in bitter cold, fighting the wind and listening to little more than the dead silence of Winter. The rookies will bail earlier, the heard will thin quicker, and the rest of us a bit more serious may finally be left alone to experience our pursuit as we ought to.

It is currently the twenty-second day of February as I am writing this chapter. The sun is shining, the birds are chirping, and the temperature is expected to reach into the 70's.

Would you please excuse me, I need to go check on the status of my dogwood.

4
.410 TIPPET

"As to shotguns, there is little choice so far as the shooting is concerned. Any good modern choke bored gun will answer—the choked being greatly to be preferred, as it concentrates its shot—which is a desirable quality in scoring—on the head or neck, the only mark for a shotgun on a turkey."

Edward A. McIlhenny, *The Wild Turkey and Its Hunting*

The unfortunate legacy of modern day technology for us turkey hunters is that we nearly feel unarmed walking through the woods with a 16-gauge, inadequately prepared with a 12-gauge chambered only for 2 ¾" shells, and if you do not have some sort of sighting system equipped to the gun such as a scope or red dot, then you really stand no chance at all. Turkey hunters a mere thirty years ago would laugh at such nonsense.

To date I have killed turkeys with twelve different guns, the majority of which have been Ithacas. Aside from my first, an Ithaca 20-gauge double barrel, all the other Ithacas were model 37 pumps. Five were 12-gauges of which three were old originals - one with a 30" barrel, another with 28", and the third cut down to 22". The other two were new pumps purchased four years ago when Ithaca Gun Company went back into business. If you consider that two different barrels were used on each of the new guns, then I have effectively killed turkeys with fourteen different weapons. The seventh Ithaca was an original 16-gauge. Needless to say, all this goes to show that I claim to shoot an Ithaca - always have and always will. It is my weapon of choice.

But I have used others and enjoyed them immensely. Of the remaining five guns, four were 12-gauges and included a Mossberg Ultimag chambered for 3 ½-inch shells, Winchester model 1300 chambered for 3 inch shells, old Fox Sterlingworth double, and old Iver Johnson single shot. The Mossberg and Winchester were fading fads, missed more turkeys than they killed, and have long since departed our ownership. Their departure ultimately led to the buying of the two new Ithacas. The Iver Johnson is old and rustic, imparting a sense of brazen ruggedness, and is two for two, far more respectable than the two departed. And while the Fox Sterlingworth is a classic, the most "turkey" gun I have used (I use "turkey" as an adjective) is an old L.C. Smith 16-gauge double. Its bluing is nearly completely rubbed off, the stock was broken completely through once, now repaired, and the overlying varnish has all but disappeared beneath the years of rugged handling. Its barrels are 26" in length and sport chokes of full on the left and modified on the right. I carried it often in my youthful years, often inquiring of my father as to which barrel should be shot first. He would tell me either, for both were "mean as hell!"

23

For whatever reason, I find the aesthetics of old double barrel, side by sides to be the most "turkey" of all turkey guns there are.

And while a 12-gauge is the preferred gun for killing turkeys, it does not mean that lessers cannot be used. Just as one-hundred pound tarpon are caught regularly on light tackle, I killed my first turkey in 1985 with a 20-gauge Ithaca double, and three since with 16-gauges. All of them died like the others; just like the one who is going to die one day to .410 tippet.

On the southwest coast of Florida, otherwise known as the sunset coast, there is a confluence of harbors and estuaries that have been given the distinction as one of the hot spots in the United States for fishing. And when referring to one very large species of fish, the tarpon, then Boca Grande Pass located at the mouth of Charlotte Harbor possesses the undisputed notoriety as being the world's best place to catch one. On record, more tarpon are caught at Boca Grand Pass every year than any other place in the world. For those who fight the tarpon, Boca Grand is a mecca.

It was March 12, 1885 when W. H. Wood successfully landed a ninety-three pound tarpon at the mouth of the Caloosahatchee River. A ninety-three pound tarpon is a mighty big fish to catch, even to us modern day technologically advanced people. A ninety-three pound fish must have been even bigger to Wood in 1885. But what made that catch special enough to be recorded for the history books was the fact that it was the first successful catch on rod and reel of what was later to become the greatest of all sport fish - the Silver King.

In 1894, a friend of Wood, John M. Roach from Chicago, bought Useppa Island and constructed one of the first ever fish camps. He appropriately named it "The Tarpon Inn" and invited all his green pocket acquaintances from the northern tundra to take part in the taming of a virgin sport. Fourteen years later, a second "Tarpon Inn" was erected on Gasparilla Island, and from there, I can only suppose the quintessence of an untamed, uncharted, rarity of sport was flushed down the toilet.

I have personally been to Boca Grand, Florida and fished its pass. I was fortunate enough to hook a tarpon there, fight him, and have him throw my hook before I got anywhere close to landing him. I was young and enjoyed every moment of the trip, but what I remember about floating in a boat in the middle of the pass leaves little desire to pursue a trip back there again. I am in no way trying to imply that I would never again enjoy being tied to a 100-pound fish 200 yards away, or floating in a boat under the warm Florida sun, in an estuary, a fishing mecca. If I ever do it again, I am sure I will enjoy it immensely. But what I will not enjoy about fishing at Boca Grand Pass is worrying about hooked tarpon, on a line attached to me at one end, getting tangled with the line of a hooked tarpon from another boat, or my tarpon jumping in someone else's boat, or even worse, theirs jumping in mine. It happens because at Boca Grand Pass, during weekends of the tarpon season, boats conglomerate in large numbers within the pass, set up spitefully close, and all sense of brazen ruggedness is lost to beer and music.

I am sure I was there at the worst time.

By the 1950's, all the mystique at Boca Grande Pass must have faded. But in 1958, off the Key of Islamorada, a new mystique was begotten. It was then that a gentleman by the name of Jerry Coughlan caught the first ever tarpon weighing over 100 pounds with the lightest and sportiest of all tackle still known to us today. He had caught a 125 pounder, with a fly rod.

The differences between fishing for tarpon in the deep waters of a coastal estuary pass and the flats around mangrove islands is so remarkable as to make you wonder if the two areas really hold the same subspecies of tarpon.

Deep fishing for tarpon in places like Boca Grande is conducted in an affair that looks strikingly similar to what any little girl or boy would draw if asked to take a set of crayons and depict a man fishing from a boat. On top of the choppy blue water would float a boat in which a man sits next to the edge and holds a rod with the line falling vertically down into the water. At the end of the line would be a hook and near the hook would be fish swimming about. Granted the child might likely miss the point that since tarpon cruise and feed at the bottom, the hook would need to dangle just a few feet off the bottom, and they additionally might miss the point that the hook would also need some sort of bait stuck on it. But that is all they would miss, and if you informed them of these two points to begin with, they would nearly depict the scene exactly.

Tarpon fishing at Boca Grande is still considered the best in the world, which may be legitimate. It does offer the casual fisher the highest of probability for catching a tarpon while additionally requiring nothing but a green pocket for boat, gas, and tackle, bait, an anchor, and two arms and hands to work the gear. Of course a hired guide may do all this work for you, short of reeling in the fish, but you still need the green pocket. What more can you get for less?

But within the ranks of tarpon fishers, there is a sub-sect that takes their cachet a little more serious than the average. Their pursuit is more serious and requires an intimate knowledge of the waters and their game with the readiness of a quail hunter. They devote years stacked on years building this knowledge and hours stacked on hours becoming successful at it. Simply put, fly-fishing for tarpon on the flats is a completely different ball game. It is the near pinnacle of all sport fishing.

Those who take fly fishing for tarpon as serious business are out on the water before the sun cracks the sky. They cut their motors, wait for the sun to rise, and then pole the flats looking for rolling tarpon. Tarpon fishers on the flats must pole their boat for two reasons. The flats around mangrove islands and keys are shallow, usually less than ten feet deep, often around five and sometimes less. Giant tarpon, those 150 pounds plus, find the deeper flats but can cruise five-foot waters easily. Baby tarpon, less than forty pounds, can be found in the shallowest, three feet or less. This water on the shallower end precludes a fisherman from running a boat with a motor, and tarpon on the flats are easily spooked, requiring near silence when hunting them. For these reasons, a pole in place of motor fits the operation perfectly.

On the flats, fishermen stalk tarpon that are daisy-chaining, rolling, and cruising. Finding them is not easy and requires an in-depth knowledge about the tides and area and behavior of tarpon themselves. But it is done, and once the foundation of knowledge is established, is actually not the rate-limiting factor in catching tarpon.

Tarpon spook easily, even to the delicate cast of a fly line should it not be presented with touch. Persuading a tarpon to take a bait or lure is a feat in and of itself, but doing so with a fly is a true challenge. But It is at this point, should a fisherman be so lucky to hook one with a fly, that the odds of landing it take a nosedive and spiral down. To begin with, tarpon have near bony mouths making penetration with a hook difficult. Secondly, on the flats, once hooked, tarpon like to jump. This jumping is largely what makes tarpon fishing what it is. Fishermen covet it; just as turkey hunters covet the gobble. Watching a tarpon jump five times in a row at 150 yards is nothing short of thrilling. But the Silver King over the water is a double edge sword, as most hooks are thrown from the mouth during the momentary back and forth thrashing out of the water. It is where the majority are lost.

Bow to the King!

I said above that fly-fishing for tarpon is the near pinnacle of sport fishing. It is only the near pinnacle because I have not further defined it. What Jerry Coughlan started in 1958 off the coast of Islamorada in the Florida Keys led to the development of a sub-sub-sect of tarpon fishers, if you will, who's obsessions and passions burn unparalleled. Theirs is the pursuit of giant tarpon with adherence to the International Game Fish Association (IGFA) regulations for fly rod and tackle. Theirs is the pinnacle, the top echelon.

Today, Jerry Coughlan's record stands a distant last in the record books. Just as records are made to be gloated, records are made to be broken, including Coughlan's, and each successor was trodden over by another, until Dr. Charles Oyer boated a 170 pounder in 1976. His, as three others before, including Coughlan's, was caught off the shores of Islamorada. Two of the other four record breakers in that time span came from the Keys, though not further specified, one was caught off Miami, and the location of the 1961, 143 pounder that broke Coughlan's went unrecorded.

Oyer's fish marked what many at that point in time calculated to be the limit. In the Keys, bigger fish were rarely ever spotted, the competition was getting thick, and the well was running dry. Most doubted a bigger would ever be caught with a fly.

In the mean time, unbeknownst to most the world of tarpon hunters, namely those who continued to pole the flats in the Keys, there remained a hidden adjunct to the west coast of Florida that would soon become and retain the interest of those seeking the biggest tarpon yet, Homosassa. As a tiny Florida west coast town, only a few knew it to harbor huge numbers of huge tarpon off its shores. Harold LeMaster, Curtis Smith, and Freddie Archibald had fished it since the Fifties and knew of its potential full well. It was not until 1977, the year after Coughlan caught his record 170 pounder, that Homosassa was discovered, so to speak, and LeMaster, Smith, and Archibald must have watched their pristine, secret flatland get over run.

Steve Huff had eaten Coughlan's record alive. He landed a 186 pounder at Homosassa, set a world record for tarpon on regulation fly tackle, though it technically never went into the books, because he declined to enter the catch with the IGFA. Huff had met all the IGFA regulations, but when he caught the record, he had been guiding a customer who was engrossed in another affair. Whatever that affair was, it was the wrong affair at the wrong time and allowed Huff to spot a giant, grab a rod, and cast to it. Can you believe he landed a world record, and furthermore, he was paid for his actions! But Huff closed the book of records from himself because he never entered it - instead, he opened the door for the world to enter Homosassa.

To date, Homosassa is still the greatest flats in the entire world to find and hunt giant tarpon with a fly. Huff's record has now been broken only three times, two at Homosassa and the third at Sierra Leone. Tom Evans caught the first in 1981- a 186 ½ pound tarpon. Brian O'Keefe did one-half pound better in 1992, but his never for a moment held the world record. For back in 1982, the year after Evans' catch, Billy Pate, set the mark at 188 pounds even, a record that still stands today.

The year is 2000 as I write this. It is puzzling that Homosassa, which is the world's greatest place to find and catch large tarpon and which produced its first world record tarpon caught on the fly in 1977, has only given up two larger tarpon in the twenty-three years since, with the largest only a scant two pounds heavier. The current record itself has been held for eighteen-years. The masses have not thrown in the towel and given up. On the contrary, the obsessions by some are so intense that they spend tens of thousands of dollars each Spring out on the flats of Homosassa, day after day, seeking not only to break the record of 188 pounds, but also pierce what seems to be the impossible, a 200 pounder.

It may be that the record will never be broken, just as George W. Perry's record setting twenty-two pound, four-ounce bass caught in Georgia is about to turn seventy years old, and no one has even come close to breaking it.

At the present, Billy Pate, who has since become the world's most famous tarpon fisher, and who still owns the world's record, once documented what has become legend among tarpon fishing circles. Pate hooked a giant tarpon, almost certainly well over 200 pounds, at seven-thirty in the morning on ten-pound class tippet. A fish weighing over 200 pounds connected to you in part by a ten-pound weighted line is no fish you can rear back on and haul in. Billy's guide, Hank Brown, poled and ran the electric motors all day following the fish around the Homosassa waters staying close to apply pressures when the time was right. As it would happen, the time was never right, and after twelve and one-half hours of fighting and an estimated twenty miles later, under the darkened skies of night, the giant tarpon broke the tippet and swam away.

While Billy Pate's story is every bit as legendary as he is, many have now documented hook ups with 200 pound plus fish only to loose them back to the sea, though nobody has come close to a twelve and one-half-hour fight. For one important and consistent reason, they have all been lost. Obsessions have been aggravated and desires burned deeper.

IGFA regulations for tarpon fly-fishing only allow a twelve-inch shock leader, usually 100-pound test. When a tarpon takes a fly deep, which is what usually occurs, the short leader is swallowed along with the fly exposing the sixteen or twenty-pound tippet to the back and forth rubbing against the fish's raspy mouth. This light tippet breaks through after so many minutes or hours, and another is freed.

These guys are so fixated on catching a giant over 200 pounds, that they will let 150 pounders, world record size not too long ago, spit a fly out instead of setting the hook. It seems that 150 pounders are fifty pounds shy of worth.

I honestly wonder if I took up the search for Big Silver, invested tens of thousands of dollars each Spring and searched for a fish 188 1/2 to 199 1/2 pounds, if I would be any more successful than these guys. It just seems they are so fascinated with the 200 pounds that they forget that 188 1/2 pounds of tarpon caught on IGFA regulated fly tackle would constitute sole possession of glorious world record. I would certainly take it.

I would gladly accept it just as I would greatly enjoy killing a gobbler with an old L.C. Smith .410 double.

Successfully landing a 200-pound tarpon with regulation fly tackle is nearly impossible, because the regulated length of shock leader is not long enough to protect to lightweight tippet to which it is attached. The weak link in the chain so to speak, or the weak link in the line to be more exact, is this lightweight tippet, and the way the IGFA has regulations set up, there is no way around it. In my opinion, that is a good thing.

The act of landing a 200-pound tarpon with regulation fly tackle is analogous to shooting a rubber band off your finger at a twenty-pound gobbler and killing him dead, at thirty yards. Both likely are not ever going to happen.

But what can happen, something I intend to do some day, and something I have come moderately close to doing once in the past, is kill a turkey with a .410-gauge shotgun, preferably an old L.C. Smith double.

I have never admired individuals who do heroic things like hunt turkeys with a bow. Thirty yards is close enough for defeat in my opinion, and I have not a mind to make the affair more difficult than it already is. Luring that old weary gobbler within thirty yards requires skill enough and should not be thrown away with a wide arrow. At thirty yards, the deal is done; the negotiations are complete, and need only be signed over the dotted line. The act of pulling the trigger and killing the turkey is the easy part, as it should be. His odds of escape at thirty yards are still great enough, for before you can even get a good shot there may still be a full bag of tricks for him to use, and in this instance the bow and arrow is a foolish gift. He does not ask for it, and he does not deserve it.

And maybe it is likewise for a .410-gauge shotgun, but I have gathered a box of 3", .410-gauge, #6, high velocity shells in case the event ever comes to fruition - and I even own an old L.C. Smith .410-gauge, side by side to do complete the act with. Both barrels pattern decent enough inside fifteen yards to be able to handle the job effectively, in my opinion, and I give it a better chance than a bow inside twenty.

Inside fifteen yards, my L.C. Smith .410 throws a dense enough pattern to consistently place three to five pellets in the central nervous system of a gobbler's head and neck. This ought to suffice, but it does not.

The inherent problem of using a .410-gauge to kill turkeys is that fifteen yards is far too short for successful turkey hunting, and effectively changes the name of the .410-gauge, such that in the hands of a turkey hunter it is no longer what it seems. It is transformed from a .410-gauge and becomes .410 tippet, the weak link in the chain.

In late April several years back, after I had killed four turkeys for the season, I courageously took .410 tippet with me to Coosa County. I was listening on the edge of a field when a turkey gobbled at daybreak across a deep hollow on the other side. As I ran down and up the other side, he gobbled to my right somewhere about the same height up the ridge as I was, and eerily closer than anticipated. In fact, when I turned, I saw him walking around an oak limb some 100 yards away, which was surprising considering the leaves were so far out. I squatted down and crawled to an old white oak behind me. The tree was wide enough to be of utility, but the bark of a white oak can be too light in color, such that sitting at its base accomplished nothing but to accentuate my silhouette. Furthermore, the timber was old, open hardwood, explaining how I saw the turkey so well so far away. Needless to say, this was not an ideal situation when using .410 tippet.

To my surprise, the event proceeded better than could be expected. The turkey flew down, shut up, and came up drumming to my left. He walked up fifty steps away (I later marked it off), never for once acted as though he spotted me, and then trotted off behind me just as a damn old spaniel came up following his trail.

Oddly, you might think, I did not get upset. The simple fact of the matter was that there was absolutely no chance that turkey would have walked up within fifteen yards of me anyway. He would have spotted me somewhere around twenty-four steps, guaranteed. On the converse, I took great pleasure in the moment, for I had the opportunity to look down the barrel of an old L.C. Smith .410-gauge double barrel, and bead a genuine Alabama wild turkey gobbler. It was magnificent!

If I ever again muster the courage to hunt limited by .410 tippet, and manage to call a gobbler within fifteen yards, I hope to be able to add the L.C. Smith .410-gauge to the list of honored weapons.

But if I continue to hunt gobbling turkeys like they ought to be hunted and not by sitting over corn or food plots or decoys, then it is just as unlikely to occur as catching a 200-pound tarpon under the current IGFA regulations.

Maybe one day when I am old and tired of shooting turkeys at thirty-five yards, I will hunt solely with .410 tippet. Maybe I will return to The Oak, my old Homosassa, and braze the wilderness and hunt like the old days. Maybe I will call one up close enough. Maybe .410 tippet will hold.

Maybe!

The author wrote this story in the fall of 2000. In May of 2001, Jim Holland, Jr. of Vancouver, Washington landed a 202 ½ pound tarpon on fly tackle certified by the IGFA at Homosassa. The author views this as a sign of good hope for .410 tippet.

5

PATIENCE

"Here, reader is the most important lesson to be learned and the most valuable in all turkey lore—patience."

Edward A. McIlHenny, *The Wild Turkey and Its Hunting*

The older gentleman looked at me and said with sure conviction and honesty, "I don't have the patience to hunt turkeys." I took his comment lightly, not thinking much of it. Oh I had heard this excuse many times before. I mostly believed in it myself. So I guess I put myself up on the high plank with all the other turkey hunters. We had patience.

It was not until I had left his house that I further contemplated his words. He had made the comment shortly after telling me a couple of deer hunting tales. And then a revelation hit me, one of those second glance revelations. I was taken back.

My father and I had discussed the very truth of the issue countless times before, oblivious to its contradiction to our central dogma. All turkey hunters believe the ability to practice patience sets them apart from other hunters, as it is taught to us by the old pros. We believe killing turkeys takes a rare and gifted talent of patience to sit still and wait a hung turkey out, to let a turkey stand there and strut at fifty yards for an hour without pulling the trigger. But if you honestly and openly examine the facts, you will realize that in the truest sense of the term, turkey hunters do not have patience - deer hunters do. And if you find a turkey hunter that does, you can bet his first love is that of the white tail.

I do not call myself a deer hunter because I do not have a passion to kill deer. But I have also sat in a tree stand enough times, fidgety and cold, to say with all the same sure and honest conviction of that older gentleman - I simply do not have the patience to hunt deer.

Let me state for a moment that I have been truly blessed with places to hunt wild turkeys in the Springtime. In most the counties of central Alabama, from the east border to the west, I have found myself at some time or another hunting gobbling turkeys. But when it comes to Fall hunting, I sadly must say that my range has been limited.

I have never experienced Fall turkey hunting in quite the same manner as those classically described Fall hunting tales, mostly because of the habitat available to me. Those classic tales took place along the river systems here in the deep south where droves of turkeys numbering thirty and upwards roamed. I have stood in similar places in the Spring and, by the number of turkeys I heard gobbling at the crack of dawn, can personally attest to these numbers. But with the ten counties currently allowing Fall hunting in Alabama, I am left with two options, Clay and

Coosa counties, neither of which harbor the massive droves of turkeys seen along these river systems. They are what I call mountain country, mountains for Alabama anyhow, and turkeys there come in groups of ten and rare small groups of older gobblers.

For the number of hours I have spent in these woods during the months of November and December, I am nearly ashamed to admit that I have killed no more mature gobblers than the fingers on your right hand. That gives you six choices (zero is a possibility) to choose from. I will leave it at that.

In my opinion, calling up a mature gobbler in the Fall is just an event of folklore long ago. It just does not happen.

Talk to deer hunters, however, and they will give you an astonishingly different report. They will amaze you with the numbers of turkeys, including mature gobblers, they see. Do not forget, these are seen in the same woods and at the same time of year that you Fall hunt. Their information is reliable, in my opinion. They have no reason to lie. If averaged out, season-by-season, we probably see about the same number of turkeys as each of them, only our sightings are those of turkey's butts a couple ten yards above the forest floor.

Deer hunters sit all morning long, and do it well. They do not thrash through the woods as we Fall hunters do, scaring off every creature on the ridge side in an ironic tale of events to find turkeys. They see nature in its norm, undisturbed, and is precisely why they get to watch mature gobblers, even these infamous hermits, walk directly underneath their stands.

My father and I, however, walk ridge tops, flush turkeys, and call up jakes. If we were only willing to succumb to the deer hunter's methods, we might get to see mature gobblers, even kill one from time to time. But we stick to our stubborn tactics and hunt Fall turkeys like they should be hunted, by busting up droves, and profess its superior nature over other forms of hunting in much the same manner football coaches say, "if football were easy, everyone would come out to play."

Last year I had a distinctly pleasurable talk with Ralph Sanders, a resident of Pickens County, Alabama. Mr. Sanders is an older gentleman, I suspect to be in his sixties, from the old school, and a heck of a turkey hunter. After chatting and sharing a few of our memorable hunting tales for a while, I propositioned him to disclose a piece of information that I deemed quite necessary to the advancement of my turkey hunting endeavors. Mr. Sanders, who may have moved slowly, boasted of killing his limit (which in Alabama is currently set at five but was six last year), for I do not know how many years running, and I wanted to know his secret. He then told me exactly what I did not want to hear, the one word I am quite disappointed in myself for not expecting, "patience." It was just like a Granny Smith apple - bitter in your mouth, good for your body, but I will be damned before I live off it.

I do concede to the truth in his statement. Patience will kill you a lot of turkeys. Sit by a green field or chufa patch long enough, and a turkey is going to come out for you to shoot. Build a blind by an old logging road and eventually you can ambush one walking down it. There is no need to even call.

The rest of his statement of faith on how to kill turkeys, can be summed up as follows. Move to your gobbling turkey no closer than 150 yards, find a seat compatible with your butt and back, call lightly and rarely (one yelp on the half-hour if he is gobbling, on the hour if he has quit), and keep your eyes peeled, for that turkey is going to show up to check you out sometime before sunset. Try it if you will, let me know how you do, but do not call me up and invite me along. I have got my own methods to iron out.

I will admit that some turkeys are so hard to kill that just such an attack is warranted - like that old pipeline turkey. Every day, he flies down in the cleared pipeline, struts, gobbles, meets hens, but in no way is willing to bend from his routing to investigate your calling.

On most afternoons you can watch him from the dirt road a good 300 yards off, and so, everyone fools around with him. And it is fun. You get to watch a show off gobbler, call to him, and analyze his response. You get to ease around the edge, stalking, trying to get closer.

But it is useless. God sees to it that he remains there morning after morning, to shame another and keep us in the humble state he intended.

After doing this for the majority of the season, the turkey eventually develops a reputation, until one morning, his latest pursuer strolls back in the camp house and declares with authority and wisdom, "That damn old pipeline turkey! He's too tough to be killed. Hell, he ain't fit to eat anyway." And so it is, from that moment on - the turkey is not fit for human consumption. No one can explain why, but if the turkey is too tough to be killed, by all reasons of logic, his muscle fibers must, likewise, be too tough to eat. But it does not matter why. The fact is, the turkey cannot be eaten, and our minds are set at ease. The turkey lives because we let it live. After all, we were all taught that you never shoot anything you were not planning on eating.

Then, one morning, your deer hunting buddy, who is finally making due on his promises to start turkey hunting, promises enthusiastically blurted out for the past five years after seeing increasing numbers of turkeys while on his stand, sits in his blind beside the pipeline. May I remind you how he so skillfully built the blind the afternoon before? He sits there waiting patiently for hours, just as he did for so many days during the Winter months, and kills the turkey. It is all done with a couple of squeaks on one of those boxes you pick up in the hunting store, strike the first note of your yelp, and see no reason to continue. You return it to the shelf like a hot potato. It might leave a residue on your fingers that could infect your good calls at home.

We turkey hunters swallow our pride and thank him for his work. Someone had to kill the turkey. God forbid if his genes were to get loose and run rampant through the county, infecting every generation of turkeys to come. There would be no more turkeys left to kill. They would all be unfit to eat.

6
HUGO AND THE HEROES OF OLD

"I have killed some turkeys. God willing, I will kill a good many more of
them. But there is a very strange and eerie phase of hunting turkeys. A phase that I
have heard discussed very seldom. A phase that is alluded to frequently, but spoken
of rarely—and that is the strange fact that it is possible to possess a turkey without
killing him."

Tom Kelly, *Tenth Legion*

Every turkey hunter who has devoted much of his thoughts to the tactics of
killing wild turkeys has his own heroes of old to claim rights to. And yet each
hunter's heroes under examination prove so little in difference as a pin oak does
from a red oak, that it is quite ironic turkey hunters use these heroes in part to define
their ideals of turkey hunting. But it is these heroes that sustain the ten and one-half
months off the battlegrounds, that mold and reshape previously held standards in
tactics, and that give life to the wellsprings within. It is these heroes that to each
gives meaning in their passion. Without them their game would dismantle to the
monotony and predictability found to some degree in other hunting sports. Others, I
recognize, that are full of pure enjoyment and well worth considerable time and
effort. Like dove hunting for instance.

Southern dove shoots are extravagant affairs with all the amenities of tasty
barbecue, lively discussions of college football, and outstanding wing shooting,
should the fields be prepared properly. The truth of the matter, as much as the
admission drags along a sense of disloyalty to my primary passion, a good dove
shoot can be about as much fun as any type of hunting you will ever do. I will not
go so far as to say that killing fifteen dove is equivalent to killing an eighteen-pound
turkey, but breaking three boxes of shells on a crisp, Fall afternoon is simply
delightful.

But the inherent problem with dove hunting, explaining in part its
inferiority to turkey hunting, is that it is a once, twice or three times a year affair.
And furthermore, since all dove act about the same and nothing all that unique
occurs when it comes to killing certain ones, it is not possible to get hung up on or
infatuated with individual dove as you can with turkeys.

Individual turkeys, on the other hand, can be known personally, and should
a hunter go into the woods more than once, twice or three times a year to hunt the
same turkey, an intimate association between man and beast can develop. For good
or bad, these relationships often extend to compulsions that perpetuate entire
seasons, or in some cases, span the course of several years.

But not all turkeys whose reputations supersede them are heroes. Take for
example walking turkeys. Walking turkeys by definition are always two-year-olds,

always come in pairs, and are no more interested in hen turkeys than they are of coyotes. I have met four pairs in my lifetime, and because of the frustration each inflicted upon me, I have elected to call them not heroes, but nemeses.

Because I spent six consecutive days chasing a pair last Spring, I have decided to designate myself an authority on walking turkeys' behavior. Through my observations, I have concluded that walking turkeys have all the hormones of eighteen-year-old boys on warm, sunny beaches, have discovered gobbling so to speak, but are utterly afraid of getting beat up by older, dominant turkeys. Walking turkeys can be followed from one side of a three-thousand acre property to the other in a few short hours, and they will gobble the entire way. Walking turkeys have a distinct distaste for the yelps of hens, which are in fact the only things they will avoid. They will cross large pastures, hop across creeks, and even fly across wide swamps should they be in the way - all of which most gobbling turkeys have a specific aversion for doing. Calling a pair to the gun is literally impossible and only serves to send them moving in the opposite direction. It is difficult to circle and get in front of them because of their speed, and even if you are successful in doing so, calling will once again only turn their direction. Walking turkeys are last heard gobbling far across property lines at ten-thirty in the morning, return just before sunset to roost in the very location in which they started the day, and set out on similar treks the next morning, albeit in a different and unpredictable direction.

Walking turkeys are hunted with enthusiasm because they gobble so much. But the tragedy is that it is not until after the hunt is over, until after the chasing of them across a property for three hours, that you realize you are even hunting a pair. It is not until after the effort is spent that you realize the inherent futility of pursuit.

Walking turkeys can become well known like heroes and can be given away like heroes, but I hate walking turkeys and hope to never meet a pair again.

But the heroes to whom I refer, do play by the rules, and the stories of a few famous ones can be read about in the literature. They carry descriptive names such as The Phantom of Possum Creek and Gallberry Joe. Heroes have tendencies towards doing things like walking up twenty steps behind you after last gobbling in front of you five minutes before. Heroes are well known for performing disappearing acts at thirty yards that would amaze even Houdini. They can fly down off roost, be heard walking certain logging roads to the same location five mornings in a row, and then mysteriously go the opposite direction while a hunter waits by the logging road on the sixth day. Heroes can be phantoms during the months of March and April, but make deliberate efforts to be seen in fields and around camp house lawns after the season has ended.

Heroes can be found on private property and only known to one person or can be the lively topic of discussions for entire groups of people sitting around country restaurant tables at five in the morning. Giveaway turkeys are often in this latter category. These heroes nearly became legends in the old days. Read Gene Nunnery's account of their fundamental importance back then.

Back in the old days when turkey hunters got together for turkey talk, the talk wasn't about how many did you kill. Rather each hunter would inquire of the others, "Have you run into any characters lately?" If, in fact, a hunter had run into a character turkey, this hunter would have the attention of all the other hunters. It is a natural thing for a good turkey hunter to want to hear of the tricks and tactics of a wild turkey who is able to outdo the hunter.

He also says,

Now back in those times when there were just a few turkey hunters and not too many turkeys, a turkey could gain a reputation. If a certain turkey was hunted and survived one season, he was on his way to fame. Fore each season he managed to survive the hunter's challenge, his fame grew. If a great amount of pressure was put on him by good turkey hunters and he still walked his domain proud and free after three years, then he became a local celebrity—a celebrity at least in the eyes of turkey hunters. To other people like young ladies, old wives, preachers, bosses, creditors, and sweethearts, he could be a downright villain. When these turkeys gained their fame and celebrity status, they usually also were given a name which became their trademark.

In 1970, five days before the close of season, my father stared down a shallow holler in The Canyon at a strutting turkey he knew well. He had met the turkey during the first week of the season and had hunted him every day after. He knew the sound of the turkey's gobble and his roosting habits, and I would venture to say that the turkey knew a thing or two about my father as well. I can only imagine the reverence that existed between the two. While my father had seen the turkey before, this particular day was different. My father had found and flushed the gobbler's hens off roost, and now the turkey paced back and forth just across a two foot wide creek for thirty minutes desperate to come find his girls—he finally did, and my father took an old friend home with him.

It seems that we all have our own characters or celebrities or heroes to speak of. Some we share, but some we do not. Meeting one and "possessing" him as Tom Kelly describes is a higher level in the game. Hugo was just such a turkey that I once knew. He was my first hero, and many Winter months were spent analyzing tactics to kill him the following Spring. But before we meet Hugo, let me first introduce you to another.

The forest where I originally set out as a boy was a vast and free expanse left deserted in the Spring, mind a few of us hunters. It was nearly a paradise, a degree I would have been fully willing to give it had turkeys been more plentiful. But scarce they were not and roaming fifty-thousand acres hunting them is hardly something to complain about.

But things changed, as they always do, so with the surge of popularity in the sport that came upon us in the 80's, we became hard pressed to set out and find new unused territory. We found the mountains of Clay County and from there embarked upon a new era leaving The Oak mostly to memories.

Clay County was mountain country, more similar in terrain to the southern ridges of the Appalachian in the eastern Talladega National Forest than what I was used to in The Oak. These hills were tall and steep, and after climbing a quarter dozen, earned the right to be called mountains in my mind. The forests were primitive with few scattered pine trees, much less so than the national forest that was slowly being converted to pine, and the territory ran deep from the roads. The turkeys in Clay County were few in number, but few enough to consistently allow us to find some gobbling and even kill a turkey or two each season. It was some of the toughest, most downright exhausting hunting to be found in Alabama, or at least from what I have seen.

Years progressed, memories of the new country were created and killing turkeys in such a land became more familiar. I grew fond of putting forth honest to God work in the finding and killing of turkeys. Working the land became almost as enjoyable as working a turkey itself.

But future seasons passed and our reach into new territory grew larger. By the early 90's, we had no less than twenty-thousand acres of pure wilderness forest, spread out across six counties in central Alabama to hunt. Twenty-thousand acres is far from the fifty-thousand we had in The Oak, but many of these places were true turkey country. By that I mean these places held thick concentrations of turkeys, and while hearing three or four turkeys gobbling at the crack of dawn was not expected, it was no less than common.

Moderation is the age-old rule, and it should do many a lot of good - those from drunkards sipping wine in back allies to CEO's analyzing data on thirty-first floors at midnight. But for a turkey hunter to turn his back on a land where thirteen turkeys were found gobbling on a single morning is asking a bit too much. Moderation looked a little too hilly and a little too thin, and Clay County as a respectable land nearly vanished from our map. There was too much work to be done elsewhere.

Four years ago, sparked in part by a desire to rekindle old memories, I revisited the mountains of Clay County. It was there that I met my second hero.

It was mid season, one of those days ordained by God for us turkey hunters, and it was all to myself in thousands of acres of deep hardwood, mountainous forests. My plan was to start at daybreak and walk all day until I found a turkey willing to gobble. I started off atop a ridge adjoining a ten-acre field in its valley. The woods were absolutely gorgeous during the mid Spring bloom. The variegated greens blended the mountainsides and were speckled with the white dogwood blooms. As the sun cracked the eastern sky, I heard one of those distant gobbles that leaves you not completely sure you had heard one in the first place, and furthermore, no clue as to where it came from. But over the next ten minutes, he gobbled several more times, enough for me to be a little bit more certain about both. This turkey was very far away, likely a mile off, and if not a mile horizontally, then easily a least mile on foot if you were to include the vertical rise and fall of each mountain needed to cross to get to him. And to further complicate matters, I was not absolutely sure the turkey was on my side of the property line. Apple pie will make you salivate from across a house, if you smell it, just as a distant gobble will charm your emotions, if you can hear it. I had heard it, and left with no better option, took off.

I headed down the side of the giant ridge, steep enough in places to almost slide down while holding on to trees for dear life. It was easy enough though with relatively little energy spent—it was downhill. But ahead lay a mountain, a giant mountain, and the turkey was somewhere on the other side.

To date, I have yet to be able to claim to have climbed another mountain of such magnitude in as few minutes as I did on that day. I nearly ran up it in less than five minutes and at the top, my legs were completely spent, barely able to support my weight. For several minutes I stood there forcing the crisp, cool air in and out of my lungs, the whoosh of my breath so loud in the quiet woods that there was no possibility of hearing a turkey gobble, even if it were sitting in a tree thirty feet overhead. Finally my lungs filled with enough oxygen to slow my breathing and allow me to take in the sound of the woods again.

He gobbled again across a second big ridge, and most likely across a wide creek, land in which I did not have permission to hunt. So I left him, a difficult thing to do, and moved on with my previous plan.

At this point, a scant twenty minutes into my intended daylong hunt, I had spent nearly all my leg's stamina. Yet, I was determined to find another turkey. I was going to continue with my plan to walk until I found one gobbling, and if that meant walking until three-o'clock in the afternoon, that was perfectly fine with me.

So I walked. I walked up ridges and down ridges. I walked along ridge tops and along creek bottoms. I walked along dirt roads and along deer paths. I walked everywhere, all the while yelping about every 200 yards and crow calling about every 100. Every now and then, I would stop and sit for fifteen minutes.

By eleven-o'clock, I had absolutely nothing to show for it. I had not seen a turkey. I had not heard a turkey. I had not even found a turkey track on the many roads I walked, or feather or dropping. But the sun was warming the air from the 50's to the 60's, the air was still, and I could not help but enjoy every moment of it.

I continued my pursuit and eased up top a ridge and into an overgrown small field. I yelped with my mouth, as I had done so many times that morning, and upon hearing nothing, as had happened an equal number of times that morning, tried my box.

A turkey gobbled close, nearly on top of me, but I had no idea of his direction. I jumped left of the field to the first tree I could find.

Silence set in for the next fifteen-minutes. Silent spells like this are nerve racking and play all kinds of heart breaking games with your mind. You simply do not know if you have spooked the turkey. Finally, he gobbled again.

The rest of the story is fairly unremarkable, as I called the turkey in and killed him, at twelve noon. He was a good turkey, too, with inch and one-quarter spurs. But it was not the kill that keeps this memory so alive in my mind. It is what I did to get that turkey. I walked miles, deep through the forests, and dug him out. I earned him.

And this is the way I wish to kill all my turkeys—by digging them out, and in doing so, earned this turkey the status of a hero, or pseudohero in my mind.

Technically, according to Webster who defines hero as "a man admired for his achievements and noble qualities and considered a model or ideal", he is no more a hero than a floater on the dove field, for neither has done anything of bravery or worthy of medals.

But Webster also defines a hero as he does all things, in multiple ways, and his last definition of a hero reads, "the central figure in an event, action, or period." In this case, he is, as all the turkeys I kill are, rightfully a hero. Webster also defines a hero as "a mythological or legendary figure endowed with great strength, courage, or ability favored by the gods and often believed to be of divine or part divine descent." While I do not believe turkeys are favored by the gods or possess any sort of deity, turkeys are figures, as we speak of them in a manner that we know them personally, and certain ones of them do possess great abilities to humiliate us people. As such, I feel a good many of them are deserving of the heroism that crowns them. Besides, Webster also defines the verb, heroize, which allows us the privilege of assigning heroism to animals for anything we personally see fit in doing so. So whichever definition you wish to follow, I rightfully crown this mountain turkey a hero, just for being deep within the forest. He was my second hero.

Now let me introduce you to my first hero, Hugo, who was more of a true hero than pseudohero.

I wish I could begin discussions here with an intricate detailed description of Hugo, such as the length of his beard or spurs, the color of his legs, or how much he weighed, but I cannot. I am unable to do so because neither my father nor I ever had the opportunity to sit down and stare at his dead body to examine such things. Hugo whipped us four years straight, and when we last heard him gobbling, I can only assume he got tired of whipping us, as it must have become old hat to him, and he moved on to bigger and more challenging feats. He is probably still out there today, whipping whomever he fancies, at the ripe old age of ten, because heroes like this do not die.

Hugo was a turkey that made himself scarce, knew when to gobble and how much to gobble, and tiptoed around in front and behind us just enough to keep us thoroughly involved in the game. His gobble was distinct, and loud, and aged to a mellow gobble by the fourth year. He could not be patterned, as I have actually found most turkeys cannot be patterned, but I state it here to emphasize that our only option was to play it his way.

We first met Hugo early one Spring morning, much too early for any turkey in his right mind to fly down and walk around. But that is where we found him, on the ground, walking.

We had first heard him across a field atop a ridge. As dark as it was, we started out for him directly across the field. As we topped the ridge and were able to hear much better, it became apparent that we were crowding him a little, and we had not walked all that far. But we were in the middle of the field and had to move some direction. Only thirty yards away, in his general direction, was a path that cut perpendicular into the woods. As it was still dark, we continued towards the path, and with fifteen-yards to go, we came face to face with an erect black object standing four feet tall, motionless, some thirty yards down the path. His silhouette was barely visible against the barren red clay that cut through the dark woods. We froze in our tracks, and all three of us watched each other motionless for one-minute.

I can only imagine at that moment in time, as Hugo met us for the first time, as he stood there studying us, that he became acutely aware of the situation and of our thoughts, and formulated his own plan. He cut right, into the woods, gobbled to let us know he wished to play, and proceeded to circle us at 100 yards, gobbling every twenty steps or so. We tried intercepting him and waiting him out and being silent and all tactics we knew of for three hours that day. Hugo won.

Hooray for Hugo!

In the third year, Hugo once dared a little, and just off roost, walked to within sixty yards of my father atop a ridge. The report I got was that his head was as blue as a Fall sky. He strolled up a fence line, in plain view, as the leaves were not yet out, causing my father to go into all that breathing and heart pounding stuff that makes turkey hunting what it is, and then suddenly turned left towards the fence, squatted down, and crawled through a tiny one-foot-high tunnel underneath. Then, he delightfully strolled away, down the ridge, gobbling and semi strutting as my father watched him do so for another 150 yards until he was out of sight and off the property. It reminds me of the rules for playing with a dog or a puppy. To keep them interested you must give them a little, like a quick bite of the stick.

Hugo always held our interest with tricks of woodsmanship and rare sightings and was always courteous enough to gobble often, keeping us afoot of his actions. And once, a week prior to the commencement of the fourth season, he permitted a ten-minute filming session, as if he were a celebrity.

A warm spell had come upon the state during the latter parts of February and had stretched into March, such that by March 12th, the dogwoods were shamefully blooming early. The redbud's bloom had come as well, and Spring was bursting wide open. Unable to withstand the temptation, my father and I had to go to the woods.

We entered a shooting house while dark, armed with a video camera, and the event that transpired before us and was captured on tape, was officially named and labeled as *Hugo's Stroll*.

Hugo just so happened to be roosting on the other edge of the field in front of us. He gobbled twice on the limb, flew down when light, and proceeded to stroll across the field, perpendicular to our line of sight, until he reached a point directly in front of us, not more than fifty yards away. It was there that Hugo performed for the camera by strutting and standing tall and pecking the ground and grooming his feathers.

We talked under our breaths about how good he looked - about how long his legs were and how they made him stand upwards of four feet, and how tight knit his beard was and how it stuck out of his breast, arching way out instead of simply hanging down, and how little and keen his head appeared. Hugo did all this, just to give us a taste, and to keep us in the game for a fourth year, and eventually strolled on by until he reached the other side of the field, where he looked back, shook his butt at us, dropped one as a souvenir, and trotted out of sight. And just for a moment (I even question it myself), I thought I heard him snicker under his breath and whistle as he trotted away.

He knew it - just as we did. The games would begin in one week.

I doubt I will ever see Hugo again, but it is possible I will, because as I said above, heroes like this do not die. If I do ever cross paths with him again, I want to be wearing an old Mexican, faded brown rug, with a hole cut in the center and hung around my neck. I want to be wearing a cowboy hat. I want to meet him in The Oak, in The Canyon preferably. I want to have a thin cigar in my mouth with smoke trailing off in the wind. I want to come face to face with him down a path. The sun will just be cracking the eastern sky. We will both stop in our tracts instantly, thirty yards apart, and eyeball each other, motionless. A far off bass drum will be pounding a slow sustained rhythm, then stop, leaving the land in deathly silence except for the wisp of the wind blowing through the long leaf pine tops. Hugo will cut right, into the woods, but this time I will be too quick. I will draw my gun and shoot him on the run. I will throw his dead body over my horse - the base drum will start back up. I will then trot out past the crater and up to the fire tower. I will smoke my cigar and relish in the victory.

Hugo will be dead! I will be the Good. Let us call him The Ugly!

7
TWO AND A DOUBLE

"It is an aloneness that is wholly free from loneliness even though as you enjoy it you are in a sense fooling yourself. You are not the last man on earth nor do you honestly want to be. It is really difficult nowadays to get more than five or six miles from somebody's house—air miles—and you hardly ever get more than a mile or two from the car. But to achieve a feeling that is so remarkably pleasant it really does not do any harm to fool yourself a little bit. I have never minded anybody lying to me if it made me feel good."

Tom Kelly, *Tenth Legion*

As the Fall fades to Winter and the first half of dove season has expired, gray skies and drab, brown forests herald the coming of the last enjoyment before the spring turkey season rolls around again—duck season. Sure, there is a second-half dove season, and the Fall turkey season cannot be overlooked. But dove hunting can never be expected to fill more than one Saturday in December and January combined, and Fall turkey hunting, no matter how much you convince yourself of its inherent dignity, can be boring as hell if I may be so frank!

For one thing, duck hunting can provide hours of intense focus stacked up days at a time before you get anywhere near water or ducks. This time is spent organizing and buying and obsessing over the one aspect of duck hunting that no other hunting sport can rival—the necessary involvement of an enormous variety of equipment. You have to have waders without holes, suspenders to hold them up, and pounds of clothes to keep you warm for the few moments before you brave the depths, take on water, and the clothes become nothing more than a cold sponge. You have to have a reliably functioning gun for the cold and wet environment and lots of shells to shoot—shells that must meet federal specifications. Infact, these regulations, federal and state, are seemingly endless and intrusive. You have to have federal duck stamps, state duck stamps, permits, hunting licenses, tables specifying the legal shooting hours for the particular day you are hunting—and a watch with you to know what time it is to obey these rules (do not forget that it must be waterproof). You have to worry about blinds, either building them before you go or taking the necessary ingredients with you to build on the spot. Some hunters, the serious ones, bring a boat along and add all the associated headaches into the equation. And decoys—everyone needs decoys. Decoys can take more time and energy than all the other aspects combined.

I used to think turkey hunting involved an overly ridiculous amount of time worrying about gathering and organizing equipment. That was before I ever duck hunted.

And long before I ever knew about the endless days of frustration that can be spent untangling jumbled masses of decoys leaving dried remnants of last year's duck weed strewn all over the floor, I dreamed of a distant, endless paradise full of ducks that was painted vividly in my mind by the words of a story my father once told. It had happened in the 1960's, somewhere remote in Louisiana; somewhere lost in the middle of nowhere and involved alligators, guns, and survival in an era when waterfowl were in more abundance than I will ever see in my lifetime.

He had been a guest on one of those high end duck hunting adventures on Pecan Island that involved plantation houses, great Cajun cooking, hunting guides and plush blinds. When it came time to leave, one of the guides he had befriended invited him to stay a few more days and accompany him to his duck club not too far away for some more hunting.

In contrast to the luxurious accommodations on Pecan Island, my father found that he had accepted three nights in a primitive, two-room shack built on a fifty-foot wide island, if you wish to call it that, rising sluggishly out of a marsh that stretched as far as the eye could see in every direction. It could only be accessed by boat and the ground of the island was hidden beneath two inches of duck feathers left over from the previous weeks' cleanings. For three days he survived off nothing more than ducks and milk and bourbon—the latter two being mixed together and drunk heavily at night.

In the mornings, under the cover of night, three of them loaded into an oversized pirogue and sped off through the maze of grass to destinations unknown to my father. After ten or so minutes, the motor quit and they came to a halt. Because the first blind was in an area too shallow to permit passage of the boat loaded with three people, and because it was not the blind to be occupied by my father, and also because he was not the boat driver, my father had to step out and wait while they took off to unload the other passenger and then return to pick him back up. He was left alone, standing in a murky marsh, without his gun, in a place unknown while both the boat motor and light got so far away that neither could be heard or seen. He says it was at that moment that fears of being stranded with alligators and eerie swamp creatures nearly overwhelmed him; and his only option was to stand as still as possible in hopes that, should one of these creatures bump into him, it would think he was nothing more than the base of a tree. When he was finally picked back up and taken to his blind, the driver had to first check the blind and run out any nutrias using it as a bed for the night.

But after all was said and done, and when the rising sun began to cast away all fears, the fruits of their labor became apparent - ducks and geese filled the sky all around them. The whole affair was an experience of brazen ruggedness blending danger and euphoria in a duck hunting mecca that to a person who covets the adventure part of the hunt (generally the tougher the better) as much as the shooting part, was awesome.

And to a little boy of seven who loved adventure, and later a teenager who loved shooting, the story which I had heard so many times became somewhat of a mystical fantasy.

By the time I got to college, with dreams of Louisiana duck hunts on my mind and a paucity of experience with such creatures that both fly and float, I wanted to go duck hunting just about more than anything in the world. I wanted to go so bad that I ended up late one January afternoon in a location that would have made an Arkansas duck hunter fall over with laughter.

Midway through my sophomore year, I was nearly a veteran turkey hunter; I had killed more than my fair share of doves through the years, and I dabbled every now and then with quail. I would have considered myself a first class hunter of creatures with feathers if not for the one void in the pattern - I had never killed a duck.

I had spent the better part of the previous spring hunting the Oakmulagee Wildlife Management Area in the Talladega National Forest just south of Tuscaloosa. Alongside one of the dirt roads that cut through the fifty-thousand acres of hilly forest, a creek running down between two ridges opened up into a twenty-foot wide pool before it closed back up and meandered underneath the road bridge. A few clumps of grass and cattails and some low scrawny shrubs flanked the pool, and a couple of rotting tree stumps rose less than a foot out of the middle.

Left with no better option and knowing full well that the probability of killing a duck in such a place was half a percent at best, I headed out and broke the water in my waders at two thirty and stood next to one of the cattails with no place to sit, no one to talk to, and nothing to shoot for three hours until sunset passed.

A one-acre clump of trees in the middle of miles of prairie farm land in Nebraska might have offered a turkey hunter better odds, and casting a tarpon rig off a pier in the Mobile Bay would certainly have been more inspiring. The set up was in such contrast to my perceptions of what duck hunting was supposed to be as to be almost unrecognizable. It certainly had no resemblance to my dreams of a Louisiana duck hunt.

But as the last few hints of light were fading off into the west, after all hope had dissipated and the gun was emptied, two wood ducks peeled over the eastern ridge, plunged down over the creek and my head at a range of twenty feet and zoomed out of sight to the west. While I may have been scoreless for the day, there was some hope, and I had a clear objective—I knew where two ducks were.

The next morning while still dark, I waded back into the pool, and thirty minutes after the sun came up, a pair of wood ducks came squealing in over the western tree line, cupped their wings, and I took them both—each with one shot.

In stark contrast to my feeble excuses for duck hunting including that January afternoon in 1993, I have been blessed with availability to prime, vast expanses of turkey country through the years. I spent my first decade in The Oak, roughly fifty-thousand acres of mixed hardwood and pine back when no one else hunted it. I have roamed several other clubs and private tracks since, many more than three-thousand acres and all with a paucity of other turkey hunters. But none of them satisfied my deepest desires like the place I found last spring.

In 1999, Scott Paper Company handed over to the state fifty or so thousand acres of prime swamp bottomland in the north Mobile Delta, just south of where the

45

Alabama and Tombigbee rivers meet. The boundaries were set, the maps were printed, and it was available to the public as a wildlife management area beginning in 2000. In February of that year, when I could be sure the woods were no longer infested with deer hunters, I drove around and scouted the limited portion accessible by car. I found that I was not the only one interested, as several others were driving around doing the same thing I was. Disappointed, because I no longer enjoy yelping to turkeys along with five other people I do not know, I was forced to find another option.

Two years prior, a friend had given me a twelve-foot, one-man duck boat designed to float in shallow marsh water that in no way was made to be motor driven. It was somewhat of a cross between a pirogue and canoe, and I figured I could use it to paddle across one of the rivers at its boundary and hunt a substantial portion not accessible by car. But I also had access to a trolling motor and figured if I could rig it to the boat in some fashion, I could extend my range considerably, albeit still quite limited. This method, I hoped, would permit more solitude in a beautiful swampy wilderness.

I knew Tom Kelly had hunted this area in the past, or at least property that bordered it and of similar terrain. So I called him later that month to propose my operation and request his opinion concerning its practicality, doability and recommendations to make the operation better or easier.

He was honest and straightforward and told me that while my operation was doable as long as the river was not up, it was not very practical, and should I be able to find or buy a real boat with a gas-powered motor, I would be far better off. I accepted his advice, decided I would heed it, and abandoned the turkey hunt by marsh-duck-boat operation altogether. Just as I started to flip through the boat section in the classified section of the paper, the phone rang.

It was Mr. Kelly again explaining that he had a fifteen-foot Delta Craft with an eighty-horsepower outboard sitting in his back yard doing nothing more than collecting leaves and pollen. He had no plans of using it until after the season, so instead of it sitting around collecting more dust, he offered it to me.

I properly declined as it was simply too great of an offer to accept, but as we continued to talk, it became obvious he was sincere and I ultimately accepted. I picked the boat up the next day.

The boat permitted me access to a myriad of rivers and slews cut in and around thousands of acres of primitive, hardwood bottomland. Cruising around and scouting and hunting left a deep satisfaction because it was a seemingly endless wilderness of primeval forest, and it was in such a primordial soup that I have always felt God initially created turkeys to live. It was as primitive and remote a place I could ever want; there were scattered cypress swamps that looked to be filled with gators and snakes, giant hardwood stands with dense, nearly opaque canopies, eerie thick vines of a caliber to suit Tarzan's uses hanging from towering limbs, and palmettos and strange tall weeds covering the forest floor. It was my long sought after Louisiana marshland, though I was using it to hunt turkeys, not ducks.

As awesome a place as it was, I ended up finding more gobbling turkeys before the season began than what I was able to find during it. But it was an early spring and though nearly all had shut up once March 20 came, two did not—two no longer with us.

I made the first one gobble on opening morning at ten thirty across a slew so that I had to run back to my boat, cross the slew, and run back up to him. After falling off a slippery log while crossing a four-foot-wide creek, I sat down amongst grasses and pitcher plants so thick and tall that I could only see the upper half of the turkey's head and neck when I shot him at thirty yards.

I continued to hunt the delta off and on for the remainder of the season, splitting my time with other more familiar areas. The turkeys in these other areas gobbled well, and I worked many of them; but the only other turkey I heard gobble in the delta occurred later in April, happened against a long list of odds, and involved water as an obstacle in almost every direction.

The difficulties began not a mile from the house when the boat trailer came off the hitch, and had the safety chains not been attached, could have been disastrous. The trailer and boat were fine (thankfully, because neither were mine), and my truck only received a small dent on the tailgate.

Forty minutes later when I arrived at the landing, I discovered the effects of heavy rain across the state of Alabama the preceding week. The river had risen several feet, close to spilling its banks and flooding the whole region. There was no way I could know if there was any land to hunt or if it was under water, but I headed out anyway.

Maneuvering Boatyard Lake turned out to be more difficult than expected because the one side bordering the river was indeed underwater making the boundaries more difficult to discern in the darkness.

I eventually made it to the Alabama River safely to find a swift, muddy current carrying loads of debris including large, dangerous logs somewhat obscured by a thickening fog. Fortunately I was heading down river.

I did my best to avoid wrecking the boat while hurrying as fast as I could because it was becoming clear that with all the delays thus far, I was late and would not be able to reach my destination and walk the quarter mile before daybreak.

I reached the head of Hogan's Bend safely and turned, leaving most of the heavy debris behind in the main current of the river. However, just a short way down, the fog became so dense that I could see no more than a few feet, not even the front of the boat, let alone the banks of the river. This posed a more serious problem than simply not being able to see where I was going and possibly running aground. At the bottom of the bend there are several successive twenty-foot-wide creeks spaced several hundred yards apart that cut perpendicular into the swamp from the river and serve to carry excess water from the interior swamps and slews to the river. In times of flood, however, they carry water from the rising river across the swamp to the heads of the Tensaw River. These creeks are serious obstacles even when the river is not up and carrying only a couple feet of water. Once I made landfall and set off, I would be confined to hunting just the area between the two consecutive creeks where I began. It was therefore imperative that I landed in the correct place to begin with, and to further complicate matters, the mouths of the creeks spilling into the river all looked about the same, even in daylight.

47

But it was not daylight nor could I see past five feet in the fog. So I cut my motor and drifted down with the current towards the bottom of the bend, hoping not to suddenly run into the bank or any other object.

At the bottom of the bend, I heard the loud turbulence of water gushing into the mouth of the first creek giving me a good measure of my distance from the bank and a plan to find the particular location I needed to land. Listening carefully for the sounds of rushing water, I tracked my progress past each successive creek, until I came to the particular creek I was looking for.

Disgruntled because both the brightness of the sky and my watch told me it was definitely past gobbling time, I tied the boat securely and hurried along beside the swift stream running down the creek yelping every hundred yards.

I finally came to a powerline hidden from view by thick weeds and briars at the edge, yelped, and a turkey gobbled directly across on the other side. I snuck through the edge and peered out into the recently cleared powerline fading out of view in both directions. With no turkeys in sight, I started setting up in the weeds along the edge hoping to call the turkey out into the clearing, but discarded the idea when it became obvious that he was a gobble-once-every-hour type of turkey. I wanted to get on his side of the powerline instead.

I eased back into the woods, ran down the powerline five-hundred yards and then zipped across after again checking that no turkey was in the powerline to see me. Half way across, I hit water flooding in from the opposite woods. I splashed across the shallow pool, found the edge of dry ground again on the other side, and began to ease back up to where I had originally heard the turkey gobble.

But long before I could get there, a hen yelped a couple hundred yards deep in the woods down by me. Just a few feet away in the woods, between me and her, a fifty-foot-wide swift current of water was pouring in from the left, parallel to the powerline, wrapping around to the right, and opening up to join the flood in the powerline that I had just crossed. This presented a new dilemma. I could either continue on up the powerline, hope to find the turkey that had not gobbled for forty-five minutes, or cross the water beside me, hunt the hen and hope the gobbler had joined her.

Another one of my peculiar fascinations has been to wade across water in order to hunt a gobbling turkey on the other side. This too stems from one of my father's stories for which he had a picture to back up his claim. It showed him with clothes and gun held high over his head, bare chested, standing belly high in a thin, shallow slew, rimmed by cypress trees. He says a turkey was heard gobbling on the other side for which there was no access, so he simply did what had to be done.

I chose to brave the water depths for the woods unknown, grabbed a long stick to help feel my way through, and took off through the current. The water made it up to my belly.

Dripping wet and my boots spilling water with every step, I came out the other side and moved forward another fifty yards only to see streams of a foggy mist hanging only a few feet over countless other currents of water running along shallow channels cutting through the swamp.

Unwilling to terminate the operation at this point, though it was looking bleak, I found one of those extremely old and tall oaks to sit at and set up facing the direction I had last heard the hen.

She answered one my yelps in a matter of minutes, and we continued to call back and forth for ten minutes when, surprisingly, the gobbler answered along with her. The hen and I continued to yelp back and forth for another ten or so minutes while he gobbled every two or three. I sat there doubtful they would ever cross the water that separated us. But they did moved closer, and to my surprise, the hen glided across, landing directly in front of me at seventy-five yards and trotted off to my right. Moments later, the gobbler followed behind, but instead of trotting off after her, he walked directly to me.

I took him at thirty yards, and he was courteous enough afterwards to flop around and land in a puddle so that I would not have to be the only wet member of the departing party.

To this day, I have yet to make it to my fantasy duck hunting paradise, to get lost in wilderness of marsh in the middle of Louisiana; but I found an equivalent place for turkey hunting in the spring of 2000.

And though I have never looked at thousands of ducks or geese filling a winter sky, the duck hunt I had back in the Talladega National Forest in 1993 ironically filled a niche of satisfaction that will forever remain atop my list of savored moments—right there along with the experience I had in the upper Mobile Delta.

Just as I killed the only two turkeys I heard gobble over the entire season in the upper Mobile Delta, I killed the only two ducks I saw over the entire season in the Talladega National Forest—two ducks that I hunted intentionally and specifically.

Individual turkeys and deer, and maybe some other big game species are hunted intentionally and specifically—but not ducks.

Since that January afternoon a decade ago, I have hunted ducks in far more productive areas. I have now killed a fair share of mallards and gadwalls, a few pintails, some green wing teal and widgeons, one blue wing teal wandering lost in central Alabama in mid January, more scaup and ringnecks than I could ever want, and countless other wood ducks. But none were more special than that first pair I killed in that paltry pond in the National Forest.

Is it possible the pair I killed the following morning were not the same two I saw fly over the night before? Yes. But it is also possible, and I would say more probable than not, that they were. And if they were, then I located and hunted and killed two particular ducks, an operation that lasted beyond the sunlight of a single day, and it is highly unlikely I will ever do that again.

8
THE OLD PRO I KNOW

"I had heard Gabe say many times that every turkey hunter meets his match when he plays by the rules. At these times a man is put on trial to see if, in fact, he is a real turkey hunter. When a certain turkey whips and humbles a man, some men will weaken and resort to unfair tactics to kill the turkey. Actually, the turkey has done the man a great favor and the dumb man can't see it. Every time a turkey out-smarts a hunter, that turkey etches the details on the memory of that man. These memories remain stored away and available when needed. Think of old ninety-five-year-old Tony McCleb and the shelves of stored memories he must have. Don't you know that he can set up on his porch and hunt again and again. He can pull out of his memory a certain turkey and play the game over, changing an item of tactic here and there to try to still outdo Mr. Turkey. Now search the memory of any man to see what turkeys are there. The ones who are there are the ones who survived man's best efforts to kill them."

Gene Nunnery, *The Old Pro Turkey Hunter*

On April 22nd of the year 2000, three days following my fourth kill of the season, I stood and watched the sun crack the Eastern sky and listened to a whippoorwill's song echo down the holler in front of me. As I listened, a great calm and satisfaction overwhelmed me. While the turkeys I had killed prior in the season were great, and in a flash I could run through the events of each in my head, I honestly wondered if the situation I currently found myself in was better than all four. If not better, then surely it was more special. For beside me, among the erupting sounds of an early morning in Spring, stood my lifelong literary hero, Tom Kelly.

During my tenure in Mobile, I had been fortunate enough to meet and become friends with Tom Kelly. I will never forget our first meeting in 1997 when I knocked on his office door overlying the Sundance Bar in Daphne. He greeted me, I introduced myself, and we talked turkey for a full hour.

Tom Kelly had long been a near idol in my boyhood, primarily based on the one book of his I had read, *Tenth Legion*. In it, he so effectively expressed many of the characteristics of real turkey hunting, characteristics to which I related through experience and for which my father had taught. Meeting my hero known only through print was a risky move, for there was the strong possibility that it could reveal a character different than the one I had conjured up based upon the words written in a mere 119 pages. But as we talked in his office, I learned my hero was indeed real and in fact, closer in opinions to my own than I had expected. We discussed woods hunting, the tragedy of field hunting, the writing of *Tenth Legion*, and the "bad old days", and he even taught me about pine versus hardwood forests

51

and their cord feet of timber too. His company was the most enjoyable turkey talk I had ever experienced. I hung on to every word he spoke.

Over the next three years I periodically kept in touch with Mr. Kelly and was always so pleased when he remembered my name every time I dropped by to talk. Sometimes I would drop by his office simply to talk turkey, which he always enthusiastically embraced, while other times I would seek out his advice on specifics, such as the snipe hunting operation I pursued in February of 1999. It just so happened that he was the world's foremost authority on snipe hunting.

But it was not until early 2000, my fourth year in Mobile when I sought his advice concerning the hunting of a new piece of turkey property that our relationship moved forward and we became friends.

The property consisted of thousands of acres of pure, primeval, swamp bottomland that could only be hunted by boat, as it was mostly surrounded by water. I had once viewed part of it briefly and knew old hardwood stands dominated. It was a property along the rivers in southwest Alabama where so many of the legendary stories of old occurred, and because I held the notion that it was in such terrain that turkey hunting was discovered, I was anxious to find a way to get in it and work it and if I never killed a turkey, I did not care.

I called him in February to discuss the operation which eventually resulted in him lending me his boat for the season.

It was in Tom Kelly's boat that I had maneuvered the rivers to get to where I hunted and killed the first and last turkeys of the season. And it was because I had his boat that we kept in contact throughout the season, and towards the end of it, he invited me to hunt with him in Clark County. I eagerly accepted.

So now we stood together at the edge of a green field on top a ridge and listened to the birds rise and sing their morning song. Mr. Kelly owled a few times and by five minutes after six-o'clock, it was apparent no turkey was going to gobble. So we split up. He sent me down the left fork in the road that penetrated the dark depths of the woods beside us, while he took the right. He informed me the road fed down the ridge east until it reached a small green field in the bottom, looped left, followed a creek a short distance, and then circled up an adjoining ridge back to the field on the edge of which we listened. We planned to meet back at the truck at eight-o'clock.

I spent forty-five minutes working my way down to the field and not having seen or heard a turkey, proceeded to head back the other side. Finally, about seven-o'clock, I made one gobble 200 yards up the ridge on the backside of the loop. I worked him well for fifty minutes, setting up in three separate locations before I realized the time and headed back to meet Mr. Kelly by eight-o'clock. The turkey's gobbles faded away to silence long before I reached the truck.

Mr. Kelly had not heard a thing and was at the truck putting up his gear. I told him of my happenings and that I knew exactly where this turkey was, that he was still gobbling, and that I could lead us back to the perfect location to call and kill him. I never expected his response.

"No—I'm not gonna gang up on a turkey. I just won't do it."

Turkey hunting has long been described as a solitary sport. It has been thus described because real turkey hunters are so consumed by their compulsion that worrying about the meeting of other hunters at four in the morning or having to find more than one adequate tree in the woods for whatever plural of the company there is to sit and hunt together only adds unnecessary interference. Real turkey hunters consume their thoughts with their pursuit and tend to be a bit narrow minded when it comes to accepting others opinions and tactics. It is not only quieter to move about the woods alone, but since decisions only require one vote, maneuvers are carried out a lot quicker too. And for turkey hunters who hunt almost every day of the season, it is simply not feasible to coordinate schedules with someone else every time.

To say that a novice or less than serious hunter will slow down a real turkey hunter is an understatement. But should two veteran turkey hunters tolerate each other enough to be able to hunt effectively together, then their combination of two separate minds and two guns working in concert double the man-power against an old gobbler and is far superior at killing turkeys than what either man can do alone. Because so many deer hunters will hunt turkeys these days, and because deer hunters are primarily social by nature, more turkeys are tag teamed and killed than ever before. It is advocated by many and praised by others, but there was a time when this was not so.

Nearly a century ago, turkey hunting was not governed by legislated seasons, bag limits, weapons and ammunition, or even the sex of the species hunted and killed. It was an era that one would assume pure anarchy ran unchecked, and to some extent, one would be correct in the assumption. Turkeys were baited and shot, were trapped and had their throats slit, were shot with rifles, and killed by the dozens on single days alone.

But ironically, it was during this era of anarchy in the 1800's and early 1900's that an unlegislated set of rules for real turkey hunting was created and refined through the ages for the rest of us to follow. Consider the following statement in *The Old Pro Turkey Hunter* as Gene Nunnery describes the planning of a hunt with his mentor, Gabe Meadow, a legendary old pro. "I knew Gabe had thought about which one of us would hunt Gallberry Joe first. I also knew it would be one of us and not both, because Gabe believed firmly in the one-man-to-one-turkey rule. The long waited announcement came as Gabe said simply, 'You'll hunt Joe tomorrow and if he survives, I'll take him the next day. We'll hunt him that way—you, one day; me, the next—until we settle this thing to everyone's satisfaction.'"

In the forward section of the book, Gene Nunnery identifies his age to be sixty-eight at the writing of the book. In the first chapter he describes his relationship to Gabe Meadow in detail and says, "We made a strange combination; a teenage boy and a man in his late sixties." Nunnery later goes on to say, "Consider the odds I had bucked: fifteen years of age, first time to try to call a wild turkey, called up this trophy turkey three times the same morning, cleanly killed him with one shot from a 20-gauge gun." Taking these points collectively - that Nunnery wrote the book at age sixty-eight, that he was taught at the age of fifteen by Gabe who was in his upper sixties, and that the book was published in 1980, then the prime years of Gabe Meadow (which I consider the ages between twenty and sixty) can be approximated between the years of 1880 and 1920, indeed a century ago for such a rule to be made. Even more likely, I say, it was passed down from previous generations to Gabe Meadow himself.

Nunnery takes great care to further describe what Gabe taught him of the old rules. He says, "As our friendship grew over the years, so did my respect for Gabe's unbending rules for hunting the wild turkey. To retain the unique challenge of real wild turkey hunting you have to be willing to give the turkey a sporting chance. Given this chance, a wise old gobbler can, at times, meet and beat the best turkey hunters in a locality season after season. You go into a turkeys domain with a shotgun and call, you locate him and challenge him, and you do your best to kill him—one on one. You do this without bait, high power scope rifles, fixed or permanent blinds, other hunters, food plots, live turkey decoys, roost shooting, tree houses, etc."

Edward A. McIlhenny thus agrees and writes in *The Wild Turkey and Its Hunting*, published in 1914, "I know of many nefarious tricks by which turkeys could be easily secured, but I shall not tell of any method of hunting and capturing turkeys but those I consider sportsmanlike. Although an ardent turkey hunter, I have too much respect for this glorious bird to see it killed in any but an honorable way. The turkey's fate is hard enough as it is."

In these days of old, people had the free rein to kill turkeys any way they wanted, and because of this free rein, some saw the value in setting down their own rules to take the meaningless killing of a bird and thus created an unparalleled challenge of pursuit - a battle. They were able to identify the unique behaviors of a magnificent creature, a king of the woods, and to set limits on his pursuit so that these behaviors may be magnified and battled against. They saw the meaning in a fair battle, and if the rules strictly adhered to, a battle that could actually be tipped in the favor of creature. Nunnery goes on to say, "A foolproof way to kill a wild turkey, I now realize, just doesn't exist and you don't want it. The uncertainty of the hunt is a fascination of the sport."

The rules of old were created in an era when turkeys were plentiful and a certain sect played the game differently. But during the dark years of the early to mid 1900's when turkeys nearly became extinct, only a fraction dedicated enough continued their pursuit in spite of the rarity of success, and they carried with them and adhered to the rules of old. No one else was dumb enough to waist their time.

I am afraid we have moved into a new era more similar to the unlegislated anarchy of a century ago than one might expect. In stark contrast, we now have strict bag limits, laws forbidding the hunting of turkeys anywhere near bait, and well defined seasons. But we have so many more turkeys now than we did a half century ago and over commercialization of the sport that just about everyone who hunts any game at all will hunt a turkey. They will erect blinds and sit by food plots or over pastures with decoys spread at twenty yards. They will call to justify their actions but then sit picking their ass and listen to turkeys gobbling in the woods a quarter mile behind them until some turkey eventually comes out and then shoot him, as if they have done something special. They watch all the videos and read all the articles advocating such methods, and while they stroke the very feathers of the dead turkey before them, know nothing about real turkey hunting.

A century ago, a minority of hunters had the guts to hold to the unlegislated rules and become real turkey hunters. They refined their pursuit, continued even as legislation brought forth seasons and limits, and became legendary old pro turkey hunters.

Today, the old pros are disappearing, no longer available to remind us of our wrong doings, and the rules of old are slowly fading from the memory of our culture. I honestly wonder if there are as many who hunt turkeys the right way today as there were in the late 1800's.

Following Mr. Kelly's response, I offered to leave my gun and not to even call, but he continued, "I'll be happy to take a nap while you go back at him, but I'm not gonna gang up on a turkey."

I humbly turned down his counter offer, expressed that I had had a marvelous season thus far and a great battle that very morning. I was thoroughly satisfied and agreed it would be best to leave him to another day.

Tom Kelly is my literary hero. He is old and wise and knowledgeable of the weary ways of a wild turkey. He is one of the few remaining that caught a glimpse of the ancient and noble era. He is a real turkey hunter, understands the game, and adheres to the rules of old. He is an old pro turkey hunter in a new century, and I have been most lucky to know him.

9

RIVERBOTTOM CHARLIE

"There is one piece of advice Gabe gave me that I want to share with every turkey hunter. Take my word for it, you can't possibly come by anything which will help you enjoy turkey hunting any more than this. Don't wait thirty years, as I did, to appreciate this gem. Gabe said, "Boy, you know or will learn, that this life is one great competitive melee. You have to compete to stay alive. It is good to learn to be aggressively competitive. There is one exception and you listen good to what that exception is. Don't you ever let the spirit of competition rule your actions toward killing wild turkeys. By this statement I mean don't get in a race with other hunters to kill more turkeys than them. Don't you be pushed by your ego and your reputation as a good turkey hunter to kill more turkeys that you really want to...You will learn that the actual killing of a wild turkey is not the final gauge of your hunting success. You will learn not to give a damn who kills what or how many."

Gene Nunnery, *The Old Pro Turkey Hunter*

One of the unique and distinguishing characteristics separating the hunting of wild turkeys from other game is that by employing various tactics of calling, maneuvering through the woods, and hiding, people can become good at killing turkeys. As in any sport, experience largely determines the success, but innate ability still underlies the threshold, and some are simply going to be better at it than others.

On a good dove shoot, anyone can kill their limit of doves, but the good shooters will break fewer boxes of shells in doing so. Deer hunters can scout for tree rubs and scrapes and hunt near these areas for presumed big bucks, but that is where the skill ends and over ninety percent do not do this anyway. Only duck hunting approaches the same category of turkey hunting in that ducks are manipulated and called in. But the approach is still distant, as ducks will easily come to calls if the set up is right with a good spread of decoys. But if you are going to hunt turkeys the right way, you are going to have to earn every kill you make with all the cards stacked against you in the first place. Unlike deer and dove hunting, you must call a turkey in - and unlike duck hunting, most turkeys do not come readily to calling. In fact, gobblers that do come in to the calls of a hen during the Spring season do so as a distinct reversal of their innate behavior. They are used to gobbling and strutting and having hens approach them instead. And to make the difficult even harder, single gobbling turkeys are pursued in areas with a disregard for other non-gobbling turkeys that likely inhabit the area as well. Unless these subordinate turkeys quietly sneak up under the gun, they are nearly ignored by hunters altogether.

Hunters who understand where turkeys like to roam, find them regularly, know just how close to approach a gobbling turkey without spooking him, maneuver on moving turkeys with success often, and have that innate ability to know when to call, how much to call, and which calls to use, kill more turkeys than those individuals deficient in one or more of these categories. This is the basis for why certain individuals who manage to kill lots of turkeys become county heroes, or, should their reputation be so glamorous, nearly earn them living legendary status across the state.

And while mastery of these skills is primarily what casts certain individuals as good turkey hunters, the measurement of their success is flawed in that it is based primarily upon the quantity of turkeys killed. The more important characteristics that truly speak of their ability, such as whether the turkeys they kill are private versus public turkeys or love sick two-year-olds versus weary four-year-olds are less often considered. Even if you do not consider those shady individuals who shoot turkeys over bait or the sloths who sit by green patches and shoot turkeys over decoys, hunters who kill turkeys in one location cannot be justly compared to hunters who kill turkeys in another, because location governs success above all other possible factors. As is the case with duck, deer, and dove hunting, turkey hunting is no different in that the numbers of the particular game pursued in a certain location and the volume of hunting pressure they feel will largely determine one's overall success, much more so than any other.

Hunters without an ounce of skill will kill far more turkeys in heavily populated areas compared with those who hunt scarcely populated areas. Situations requiring hunters to choose which turkey to hunt when multiple are heard gobbling on roost are a luxury and far more ideal than chasing distant, lone gobbles nearly a mile away. And turkeys who are locked behind gates, gates opened only a few times during the season, are a hundred fold more responsive and willing to come to calling than those cornered on four sides by hunters four out of five days for six weeks straight.

If you wish to artificially categorize turkey habitat, two broad groups can be considered. Though ample room for sub-categorization within each group remains open for discussion, hill country and blackwater swamp bottomland sit across a wide and distinct line from one another such that hunting turkeys in one location can be surprisingly different from hunting turkeys in the other. Turkeys in these two locations may exhibit the same behaviors, but the lay of the land dictates entirely different operations in pursuit of them.

The blackwater bottomland along the major river systems in Alabama, including the Black Warrior, Tombigbee, and Alabama rivers, have one overriding and supreme characteristic making them superior to hill country in that they can hold amazingly high populations of turkeys. In all fairness, this characteristic is not limited to turkey populations alone. Everything in this sort of bottomland comes in more abundance, both game and non-game species - deer, squirrels, raccoons, snakes, and bugs to name but a few.

I once got two turkeys gobbling at three-thirty in the afternoon not 100 yards away along the Black Warrior, and when I called a hen away from them in less than five minutes, I thought it would be over in less than two. But they never came in. In fact they stayed out there between 100 and 200 yards gobbling at every noise I made until seven-o'clock, flew up to roost over a swamp, and it was the most miserable afternoon I have ever spent in my life. The mid-April afternoon was blistering hot, so I had worn extra light, cool clothing. Regrettably though, I had forgotten to spray myself down with insect repellent. To say that a swarm of mosquitoes attacked me that afternoon is a poor choice of words. It was more like an army than a swarm. And because turkeys can usually see you through 100 yards in open bottomland, I was overly cautious and did very little to swat the hundreds of mosquitoes attacking my blood filled body for three and a half hours. The hell with comfort when it comes to killing turkeys I say.

If any of you ever get caught in a similar situation, pay attention, for I have some hard-earned advice for you. Three and one-half hours of ravenous, blood sucking demons attacking your body while listening to turkeys gobbling 150 yards away is enough time for you to think up all sorts of stupid solutions that seem clever at the time. Allowing an entire swarm of mosquitoes the uninhibited freedom to feast on your body for thirty minutes in the hopes that they will eventually fill up and leave you alone does not work. Their reserve forces are far too numerous, and at the end of the operation they are just as veracious as the start. Furthermore, allowing individual mosquitoes to completely fill their body with your blood in the hopes that in doing so, they will suck out all the itchy chemical they injected to thin your blood does not work either. I watched one mosquito fill his back side with so much of my blood that after he stopped feeding, he could not even fly away. I finally nudged him with my index finger and he rolled off and fell to the ground. Unfortunately, his bite itched for the next solid hour.

Along the Black Warrior, I have been amazed by the number of deer tracks that can be counted in close proximity while sitting at a tree calling a turkey. These are the same locations where 200 plus doe tags are given each year for five-thousand acres.

The food available to game species there is so plentiful as to be astounding and can support these large herds of deer and droves of turkeys.

I once heard eleven turkeys gobble at the crack of dawn along the Black Warrior and could have easily hunted any one of them. I have turned the corner of roads into fields only to watch twenty-five turkeys run away in late April - droves larger than you find in Clay County in December. Blackwater bottomland turkeys also have the distinction of gobbling more than hill turkeys, gobbling earlier in the season than hill turkeys, and gobbling earlier in the day than hill turkeys such that they are nearly gobbling when it is technically still night.

Stereotyping is a sure way to be discredited in this politically correct society, and no doubt making vast generalizations can result in the same. But generalizations can reveal a pattern of truth and be somewhat useful in categorizing information such as productivity of turkey habitat. And it is for the reasons stated above that in my opinion (yes, this is a generalization) killing turkeys in blackwater bottomland is easier than killing turkeys in hill country because it usually has more turkeys. This is purely opinion, of course, and I am quite sure many would fight me in protest. There are no doubt individuals who have not enjoyed the success I am alluding to while hunting along the Tombigbee or Black Warrior or Alabama, and I am sure many of them are cursing me right now - so be it!

Detestable individuals who boast about killing two turkeys with one shot are not twice as good of hunters as those who let pairs walk for fear of killing both - they are half. Turkeys who are killed over decoys in fields by persons who fill their limit in doing so are not honored but defiled. And legends who kill their limit every year in private blackwater bottomland with a good mixture of fields and openings to hold turkeys; who hear five or more turkeys gobbling on roost, even if they honorably pursue, call, and kill turkeys cannot be compared with unsung heroes who kill one or two turkeys per season in thousand-acre wood tracts of hill country, especially if these turkeys are characters for which the hunter has spent the better part of one or more seasons pursuing.

This is not all to say that killing an eighteen-pound turkey along one of the major river systems in Alabama or other blackwater bottomland is not an honorable feat. It is - if done correctly. But digging turkeys out, I mean really having to work for one, hill country or bottomland, leaves a far more sustained satisfaction in your memory.

Spring turkey hunting in the late eighty's and early ninety's experienced an explosion of hunters of which a large portion were deer hunters. I can only suppose their influx is chiefly responsible for the occurrences of the egregious big turkey contests that all hunting stores have now a days. Contests such as these, in truth, are actually more suited for deer, but the scoring system used for judging turkeys certainly is ingenious. If you consider that twenty-pound turkeys, ten-inch beards, and one-inch spurs are the thresholds of what we consider trophies, then weighting the beard by a factor of two and the spur by a factor of ten each (twenty combined) is a marvelous way of normalizing these three factors. Adding these three properly weighted factors results in a score that can be used for ranking turkeys in a contest. The score of the prototypical twenty-pound, ten-inch-bearded, one-inch-spured turkey would be sixty.

In addition to some individuals who enter these contests to win prizes, other egocentric individuals view them as a wonderful justification to have their picture while holding a turkey plastered on the hunting board for everyone in the county to see.

Personally, I would never succumb to such as temptation, as I was properly raised as a child. Just as the measurement of good turkey hunters is flawed, comparing turkeys based on a physical calculation excludes the quality of the kill. I would rather kill a sixteen-pound, six-inch bearded turkey, as long as he gobbled and I legitimately called him up than a twenty-two pound turkey with a twelve-inch beard while sitting over a green patch. If you want to know the truth, I hardly care about the weight and actually prefer long legged, seventeen-pound turkeys that stand four feet tall. They seem to epitomize the slim and sleekness that defines the species. There was a time when nineteen-pound turkeys were giants and twenty pounders were unheard of.

Turkey scores displayed on hunting boards measure characteristics learned about turkeys after they are killed and say nothing at all about the important stuff that really matters while they still walked.

But for reasons beyond the flawed nature of the scoring system, I will never enter one of these contests because I was taught never to boast about killing turkeys or tell others how many turkeys I have killed. The temptation to boast about the number of turkeys killed in a season can be overwhelming, especially during those years when you get really lucky and kill four or five. And should a hunter give in to this temptation, it can lead him to start killing turkeys for others, primarily to perpetuate his own reputation.

The best hand is not to play at all and keep the numbers game to yourself. If you want to know the truth, this tactic can absolutely drive other hunters crazy. Should another hunter ask you how many turkeys you have killed, be honest about not killing any if you have not. But if you have, whether it be one or four, simply tell them you have had a fun season, that you have heard some good gobbling and worked some difficult turkeys, but that you have also had a little success too. But do not tell them how successful. If they are the type to play the numbers game, this type of answer will absolutely strangle them with curiosity. Even if you have only killed one turkey, they will think you have killed more.

For the past decade or so, Paul's hunting store just outside Tuscaloosa has held one of these turkey contests each Spring for the hunters in Tuscaloosa, Green, Hale, and surrounding counties that border the Black Warrior River in central Alabama. For several years, one individual has consistently shown up on the board more than any other, and by the end of each season, he is usually up there at least four or five times. In every picture, he wears a Frankenstein sort of mask with a wig and a full brimmed, camouflaged hat. He goes by the alias Riverbottom Charlie, and his hidden identity is one of the slickest schemes I have ever witnessed.

Riverbottom Charlie must be one hell of a turkey hunter, for he kills or nearly kills his limit every year. Riverbottom Charlie has perfected a method to boast about all the turkeys he kills while keeping his identity hidden. Riverbottom Charlie is a legend, yet we do not even know who he is.

The creation of Riverbottom Charlie was ingenious and would have been perfect had he not made one mistake - the name gives him away.

If I get up the nerve, one day I am going to buy my own horror show mask, wig, and hat and use them to enter my own turkey in one of these egregious contests. It will be imperative that I do so only after killing a real character - a hero who is old and wise, a hero in the likes of Hugo and Gallberry Joe, a hero that I truly earned. I will put on my disguise, enter the store, and show off my turkey with all brashness of a deer hunter who just killed his first—one that just so happened to be a twenty-two pounder with a twelve-inch beard and one and a half-inch spurs. I will have my picture taken and mounted proudly on the board. When they ask for my name, I will say the following.

"I am a deep woods, hill country turkey hunter who stays away from the likes of green fields and chufa patches. I am a proper turkey hunter who would never lower his standards in morality and use items such as decoys. I hunt turkeys in locations that require work to find them, and I hunt them one on one. I only shoot the ones I call up and only the ones who gobble for that matter.

"You see, this here sixteen-pound turkey won't score well in your books, because he is light on your scales. But I can assure you that for what weight he lacks on the scales sits ten times heavier on my heart. This turkey is an old foe, and I hunted him for three years straight. His spurs are long and sharp as testament to his age. He was a wise turkey with an endless bag of tricks. I knew him well. I respected him. But in the end, I defeated him.

"I am a real turkey hunter, mastered, and follow the rules of the old pros. I am a throw back to the days of old, and I am deadly.

"What shall you call me? How about 'Hill Country Johnson'."

10

DROPPINGS

"A creature who is normally the epitome of slim, sleek alertness, whose feathers lie close to the body, smooth and luminous to the point of being burnished, who normally moves as if all his joints were oiled, turns all of a sudden into a clumsy ball. Every feather looks as if it had been plucked out and then glued back on, wrong side to. The neck, which had a sinuous, flowing and nearly serpentine grace is cramped back into his shoulders in the posture of a retired eighty-year-old bookkeeper with arthritis."

Tom Kelly, *Tenth Legion*

As I begin to think about the information I am about to present, and ponder exactly how it is that I am going to reveal it to you, I sense the need to begin with a disclaimer. I am fond of wild turkeys, particularly the *silvestris* subspecies. I like their tall, dark, slim appearance. I like the fact that the feathers on a gobbler's neck give way to skin. No ordinary skin, mind you, but skin that changes between three vibrant colors - red, white and blue. I like the dark brown colors on a gobbler's breast feathers that reflect iridescent purples and greens and blues in sunlight with a strip of black at the tip. I like the length of a turkey's legs with that pinkish red color. I even like the way turkeys sound, especially when they gobble. I wish I could say I like the way turkeys act, but I have been humiliated all too many times for that to be a completely truthful statement.

I am a turkey hunter, and for this reason, am a little peculiar. I may not seem so to many of you reading this book, for you, as such, fall into the same category. But being a turkey hunter, by definition, places us in a class that is somewhat different from the general population. We think and act peculiarly different from others. Be that as it may, I am neither going to apologize nor try to make gutless excuses for my actions.

Nearly a decade ago, in early February, a prolonged warm snap had gripped the state for the better part of two weeks. The birds were singing with the crack of dawn, and an occasional daffodil had opened its blossom. The sky was blue and afternoons warm enough that the breast of Spring could easily be felt. With the three months of a gray Winter passed for an individual who covets the fullness of a Spring, like a turkey hunter, resisting the draw to the woods was a near futile act. My father and I headed out the next morning.

An hour after sunrise, we left the truck at the head of a dirt road and ventured down it into the depths of the swampy bottomland along the Black Warrior river. Two-hundred yards ahead laid a thirty-five-acre green field bordering a cypress-laden swamp that turkeys absolutely loved to roost in. As we approached the field and peered about the outskirts of trees, searching for anything of enjoyment to watch, we found three mature gobblers curiously strutting about the far corner. I was quite surprised, as I had never been aware that turkeys were up to these sorts of activities in early February, nearly a month and a half before the Spring season was to commence. Such actions are valid in March and April - but not February. Furthermore, the previous Fall season had only recently ended, and gobblers were no more interested in the whereabouts of hens then than I am of moose hunting now.

If there has ever been anything of praise to credit deer hunters with, it is that they possess a rare and gifted talent for the building and maintaining of two things - green fields and shooting houses - and both are invaluable to a turkey hunter who wishes to relax and view turkeys before the season commences. This was precisely the situation we found ourselves in. We slipped into a stilted house on the edge of the field and relaxed on the padded bench with carpet at our feet and turned on a little butane heater for warmth - you know, all those things deer shooters get to take comfort in. We lazily gazed upon the three strutting turkeys ease from the woods to our left out into the field.

It is a delightful situation to be able to just sit and watch turkeys and not have to worry about sneaking around and trying to kill one. Without the pressure, it is almost as if you enjoy it more - almost. So we sat and chatted and dreamed of killing one of them at a later date, and even discussed which one we would kill, as if it mattered.

As the turkeys continued to strut and half strut and piddle about, an additional group of turkeys came out from across the other side to meet them. There were thirty-one of them to be exact, most of which were hens. The two groups joined up, all the flagrant nonsense ended, and the focus of the party shifted to dining on the grassy needles below. They purred and clucked and pecked around and lightly yelped back and forth - it was a cocktail party if you will.

Two distinct clicks of gobblers emerged among the party. Mingling with the hens near the left side were four jakes, and clear across the mass, a few steps set off the group, the three mature gobblers kept to themselves. All the other turkeys were hens, except for one. Far in the back of the group, hidden behind the backs of the hens and jakes and other gobblers, was a lone turkey that I only occasionally caught a glimpse of, and I thought it just might be another gobbler.

The piddling continued, and we enjoyed watching the whole affair through the binoculars. Then, at a moment while I was intently looking for things like hen beards and gobbler spurs, the whole group suddenly split apart, right down the middle, from rear to front, as if someone were unzipping them, and the meanest gobbler you ever saw strode right through. As he advanced, the group joined behind him, as if zipping back up, and when he cleared the other side, the halves were fully rejoined again into one confluent mass. It was just as if Moses was parting the water. He did not have to bully his way through by pecking or slapping others with his wings. He simply decided to cross to the other side, for whatever reason that compelled him to do so, and no hen or jake was about to be caught standing in his way. This gobbler was a king.

As I said, he was mean looking. That statement may strike you a little funny if you have not seen many turkeys as I have. But turkeys do have personality traits that can be expressed through physical characteristics. His eyes were narrow and his beak pulled tight, and at this point, I am at a loss as how to further describe what it is about a turkey that makes one look mean. You will just have to trust me on this one. Is it not possible to instantaneously perceive the temperament of a dog before it has uttered a growl or curled its lips to snarl? It is, just as you can with elementary school teachers and drunkards in back alleys. It is not any different for turkeys?

Later that March, I went back to that same area and killed that very same mean gobbler. How do I know? I know because before I shot him, he stood at fifty yards and strutted for forty-five minutes, allowing me ample opportunity to study him and his facial characteristics and get to know him, so I can tell you with surety and honest conviction, it was the same mean as hell gobbler I had seen parting the waters over a month earlier. He was magnificent.

Later that season, I found a picture of a gobbler on a turkey call package that looked exactly like him. I wondered if the turkey I killed really had been a king, and the paparazzi had found him before I.

I liked the way his head looked so much that I kept it frozen in a zip lock bag for two years. No I am not crazy, and I definitely do not partake in satanic rituals. I just enjoyed looking at it on those monotonous Winter days and recollecting about turkey hunting days past.

Might I remind you that deer hunters do the same thing with their kills, only they are far ruder and hang the damn heads all over the walls of dens and hallways. Even more so, they pay someone to have them all fixed up so as to look alive, and when you walk in a room with a few, you get the eerie feeling that you are being stared at. I did no such thing here and proclaim that I am not all that crazy!

Frozen turkey heads are not the only strange objects to find their way into our freezer. Back in The Oak, deep in The Canyon, we once found a gobbler dropping so large, that we were somewhat terrified to be in the woods. To help you understand the size of this dropping, let me say that it took a full size hand, not palm, but hand, from the tips of the fingers all the way to the wrist to support it. If you are wondering as to the credibility in my observation, I appreciate your concern. But through the years, I have probably seen a good many thousand turkey droppings to know gobbler poop when I see it. It was classic in appearance - it had the typical "J" shape, though somewhat knotted at the end. I estimated its size to be roughly four to five times that of a normal gobbler dropping, and we had found it in the bottom of a hollow in the middle of fifty-thousand acres of forest land. I can guarantee there were no barnyard turkeys nearby to drop it, or corn products available to produce it. This had come from a genuine, southern, Alabama wild turkey gobbler.

My father and I stood around it in awe for a good ten minutes discussing its very existence, and pondered its creation. Was this to be expected of a giant gobbler, upwards of sixty or seventy pounds? That question was answered later in the season when we found three similar droppings in the same area. I sure wanted to get a chance to see that gobbler, but if his droppings indeed reflected the size of his body, I was unsure whether my sixteen loaded with number sixes or even my father's twelve would be enough.

These droppings were truly a sight of amazement, and as such, we could not just let them decay back into the soil never to be seen again. This was a scientific discovery, and we had turkey hunting friends who could appreciate their magnificence. So we carefully picked them up, situated them in our coat pockets as best we could without breaking or flattening them, and brought them home.

Again, for those of you unfamiliar with turkey customs, turkey droppings are neither smelly nor disgusting. In fact, it is quite common for a turkey hunter to pick up a dropping to test its freshness. All the books and articles tell you to do so, and if it is still warm, then he is not all that far away. In theory this should work, though I do not think it has ever changed my course of actions even as much as an inch. But I continue to do it, and suspect there will come a day when I discover a warm dropping steaming in the chilled air, and I will look up and see its maker at thirty yards. I will shoulder my gun and shoot him right there and then write about the great utility in checking things such as turkey droppings.

We were proud of our findings, and so kept our specimens for a detailed study. My mother, however, felt a little differently about their importance when she found sandwich baggies full of turkey poop in her freezer.

Although the gobbler droppings we found that season were truly amazing in their own right, we have since seen another that to this day defies all logic. It was in the same national forest, only this time we did not find it in the middle of the woods, nor while walking on a dirt road. We actually spotted it from the truck.

It was mid afternoon and an exceptional day to be turkey hunting. We were slowly driving down a single-track dirt road when a strange object up ahead captured our attention. As we got closer, we could make out some sort of tracks leading to and from it. It warranted a closer look.

We stepped out of the truck and were confronted with such a foul odor that I turned and gagged a couple of times. It was poop, no doubt about it. Without getting into a gross description, I can tell you that this dropping was close in size to that of a banana. If I had found it in the woods on top of dead leaves and grassy shoots, I would have credited its maker to be a large dog, bear, or even another turkey hunter who just could not hold it any longer. I have laid similar ones in the woods myself. It is just a natural part of turkey hunting - laying one down that is.

But this was on a dirt road, and it had rained the night before. These were not deer, bobcat, dog, or even human tracks leading to it. These were turkey tracks, and even more dumbfounding, those of the female kind.

Our first response was to analyze the scene for human fraud. We certainly did not want to become the recipients someone's foolish prank. If we were to speak of it later, we had to be absolute about the authenticity. No one was going to believe us anyway, but I was not going to throw away my reputation on another's senseless act.

The road was covered with slick mud, as it had rained the night before. No disturbances, except for the hen tracks, could be found for 100 yards in either direction. So, either an ostridge with his ten-foot wingspan somehow learned to take flight, made his way over from the Birmingham zoo, and dropped it directly in the middle of those hen tracks, or a fourteen-pound female *Meleagris gallapovo silvestris* walked across and did. Since I have not seen any ostridges soaring around this area, or ever soaring for that matter, I must conclude it was the latter.

Imagine how good she felt afterwards.

11

SLOW DEATH AHEAD

"There are many theories as to why a gobbler will sound off at the owl's hoot. Some say the owl is the turkey's enemy. Gabe said this ain't so. The reason he gobbles at the owl is quite simple. It's the spirit of competition. The vain, egotistical gobbler thinks his gobble is the most wonderful sound of the forest."

Gene Nunnery, *The Old Pro Turkey Hunter*

Small towns in the rural Deep South have a prestige for holding strongly to traditions which more than slightly deviate from those of the rest of the country. This is portrayed yearly in Hollywood films and involve gossip, religious affairs, and ignorance run unchecked. Most are pure fables of old. We do have electricity in the South, have had it for the better part of the Twentieth Century, and all women do not sit around in slinky cotton dresses under a fan, sipping tea, with sweat dripping from the brow to the bosom. These inaccuracies are not a cause for too much concern, for that which is good and remains undiscovered is all the better. Less the sweaty blue-eyed blonds, the portrayals are effective at perpetuating Southern stereotypes and keeping Northerners the hell out.

Small town Southerners still retain a sense of dignity and belief in God. Any vegetable or meat or bread that can be fried for supper is done so, routinely. And teenagers fill their Friday and Saturday evenings by cruising the town in their supped up trucks or hot rod Trans-Cameros. These activities serve as but a few examples of what I know to occur off the beaten path, but I am only being half honest. Because the Deep South remains largely segregated (not government sanctioned mind you), both white and black folks proceed through life surrounded by friends and colleges primarily of the same color. It is for this reason that I am far less aware of the daily lives and customs that take place among the black rural Deep South. I simply have not had the same opportunities to witness their lives. But once, I was afforded a rare glimpse into their world that was sort of a gift, and I cherish its memory to this day.

Three miles outside a two traffic light town in east Alabama is a 300-acre farm that my father and I have had the privilege to hunt for the past decade and a half. The property is far from ideal in the eyes of a turkey hunter: has just enough acres to barely fill a morning, and has only a reasonable number of turkeys. But its primary lure is the accommodations - a luxurious cabin overlooking a ten-acre pond full of bass and brim. Ponds such as this one can provide perfect fillers for those late mornings when you happen to quit early because the turkeys are not gobbling, or should you be so blessed, happen to kill one early. I lie not when I say that there can be few things more enjoyable in life than to sit in a boat on a pond surrounded by turkey woods bursting to life with dogwood blooms scattered about, on one of those gorgeous mid-Spring days, slightly chilled but not cold, under a rich blue sky, all after having killed one that very morning. It is a rare and grand experience. I have done it twice.

Just inside the two great rock columns marking the gravel road entrance to the property is a small garden now growing corn and okra and other vegetables and marks the memory of a family departed that we once knew. Though now torn down and hauled away, there once stood in its place an old, dilapidated, wooden house that could have been taken right off the screen of one of those unjust Hollywood films greatly exaggerating the deprivation experienced by the poor in the South. It was a two bedroom, one bath, wooden shack with a small kitchen, small dining room that doubled as a living room, and walls covered by faded, gray paint flaking off substantially in most areas. Its floors were not even finished, and doors hung desperately to single hinges. A wooden porch preceded the entrance, lined by a wood railing and decorated with a wood swing and two wood rocking chairs. Sheets of rusted tin on the roof buckled under the hell-hot southern sun, lending concern for leaks, and sheets of green roofing shingles constructed as makeshift siding were faded, weathered, and nearly falling to pieces. In fact, whole sheets had fallen off on the southwestern side. The house was set upon one-foot brick pillars, and from underneath, groves of thick briars grew out. Combined, the house and porch could not have encompassed more than 750 square feet. It was in this dilapidated shack that Louvelle, Willi, and Willi D lived far beneath a modest existence.

Willi and Louvelle were more than pleasant folks and always eager to greet us at the door. Their age was climbing into the upper seventies, and Louvelle's health had been deteriorating fast for the past several years. He spent his last years nearly blind and did little more than pass the days on the porch listening to cars go by, rocking in one of the wooden chairs. Willi D., their son, was a quiet, content man whose height could not have exceeded five feet. He was deformed and walked with a wide set staggered gait. His left leg must have been a few inches longer than the right so that when he stood, it cocked sideways and bent at the knee. His bottom jaw jutted out, the result of a gross under-bite. Just like his parents, Willi D. was pleasant and cheerful and always eager to greet us at their door, but his speech was absolutely incomprehensible, creating a distinctly uncomfortable atmosphere whenever we were left alone together, albeit only for brief periods of time.

The Todds were decent folks, and we stopped every time we hunted to say hello. One Spring morning, the Saturday before Easter Sunday, we stopped the truck in front of the house, stepped out, shut the doors, and encountered a distant harmony filling the air. The harmony was splendid and grew louder as we walked closer to the house. Inside, there must have been ten people gathered together, singing praise like none I had ever heard. The closer we got, the more spiritual and beautiful it resonated. It was wonderful. As we took our first step up the porch stair, my father and I hesitated, looked at each other, and without speaking a word, read each other's thoughts. The affair was too spiritual and inspirational and beautiful for us to disrupt. So with that thought, we turned around, walked away, and drove off - I do not believe we spoke a single word for the next quarter hour. The Todds never even knew we were there. I can still hear the music today.

The year after, Louvelle died, and we received an invitation to his funeral but were unable to attend. The invitation was a white church like program with a picture of Louvelle on the front, and above in bold capital letters read the title, "A HOMEGOING CELEBRATION."

Apparently in the Deep South, rather than conducting a sad remembrance, the poor and black pay final tribute to their deceased in music and praise and celebrate their God granted moments spent with the beloved individual. And if the song at the gathering was anything similar to our experience that Saturday before Easter, then I can only imagine a wonderful remembrance it would be indeed.

Several years later, my father and I crossed paths with a gathering of people that I can only conclude was one of those "homegoing celebrations." They were on the lawn of a seventy-five-year-old brick house. It was warm, and Spring was in its finest color. The gathering consisted of twenty or thirty black folks, both young and old, most decked out in dark suits and black dresses. They appeared somewhat joyful, not saddened, and stood about in clusters of five or ten. Thirty yards up the road, before we had rounded a curve and seen them, a sign had been erected in the middle of the road. It had been placed directly over the double yellow line and permitted passage on either side. Its purpose was a warning, and in dark capital letters read, "SLOW DEATH AHEAD." Had I not read the sign before I saw the gathering, I may not have known what the group was gathered for. But I had, and I could only figure that I had indeed witnessed a real life "homegoing celebration." But as I passed by and viewed the event, my mind was contemplating the strange sign.

Urban neighborhoods with close set houses and young families invariably have yellow caution signs erected alongside the roads that read, "SLOW CHILDREN PLAYING." Since signs do not come edited for grammar, the meaning of this particular sign is meant to be read with a comma after the word, slow, or "SLOW, CHILDREN PLAYING." In other words, slow your speed, for lots of little children frequently play in this neighborhood. But since the comma is left out, for whatever reason, it is at your will to read the sign with or without commas inserted and to interpret it however you wish. And if you should happen not to insert the comma, then you cannot be faulted with the erroneous interpretation that slow children in this particular neighborhood can often be found playing together. The thought of this particular interpretation is enough to send kids into fits of laughter at the thought of children running around and throwing balls and yelling, all in slow motion. And as brutal as kids are, they often stretch this imagination and giggle at the thought of a neighborhood full of mentally retarded children gathered together for a game of touch football.

Before I ever rounded the corner and witnessed the homegoing celebration, it was in a similar struggle of interpretation that I contemplated the words, "SLOW DEATH AHEAD." To be perfectly honest, I wondered if the death to which the sign referred was a tall, shady character cloaked in black carrying a long staff with a sickle blade. Could the death referred to have been The Death, Mr. Death or Dr. Death, or whomever you wish to call the man who will meet you in your last moments of life to carry you away? Could the sign have been a grave warning to proceed with extreme caution, for up ahead, around the curve, Death was lurking in the shadows, hiding, and if your steps were not careful enough, then he just might step out and take a hold of you.

I spoke all my thoughts to my father, and we laughed and later concluded the sign ought to have read, "SLOW, DEATH LURKING AHEAD." We still speak and laugh of it today.

It was several years back, a full two weeks into season, when my father and I made a turkey gobble across a swamp in a property adjacent to the Black Warrior River. The northern side of this 100-acre tract was bordered by a distinct fifty-foot ridge which arose from classic, flat, bottomland below and flanked on the western and eastern sides by two swamps. The river weaved its way in a net southwestward direction, marking a somewhat serpiginous, southern border. The swamp on the western side emptied though a small feeder stream into the most southern portion of the river, was longer than wide, and ran abrupt with the foot of the western corner of the northern ridge. A metal grated bridge connected the relatively isolated tract to the rest of the property across the small feeder stream a good 125 yards from the river. A dirt road proceeded from the bridge up a small embankment that contained the excess water in times of flood and ventured out into the dark, matured hardwoods that so characterizes classic swamp bottomland. From the stream it ran not fifty yards before terminating into right and left turns that looped and connected the inside edge of the tract defined by the borders above.

It was shortly after ten-o'clock when he answered our yelps, not more than a few steps after crossing the bridge.

His gobble sounded somewhere in the direction of the northwestern corner, likely within the vicinity of where the swamp and ridge ran together. He did not sound close, but as the foliage of swampy land always precedes the hills, the leaves were far past half out. Taking this into consideration along with the open woods that so characterize this type of forest, excessive movement was a precarious action. So we eased up another twenty-five yards, picked a couple of trees, and set up.

We worked the turkey for an hour, though he had hardly gobbled ten times and only once seemed to venture closer than 200 yards. By eleven-thirty, he shut up and paid us no more interest. By noon, we gave up on the deal, walked the loop, and called it a day.

The next morning found us atop the western corner of the ridge at the crack of dawn. He gobbled at five-o'clock within the confines of the loop below while still dark, eventually flew down, and we chased him around for the better part of the morning. This particular turkey was one of those characters you occasionally meet who has the propensity to take off in the opposite direction from which you call, no matter how many times you move and circled to get in front of him, and he was always courteous enough to gobble as he went, thus letting you know exactly where he was and which direction he was going. The event left us honestly wondering if we would be more successful by not calling at all. The possibility of better odds must be considered if you were to sneak in, say nothing at all, and hope he blindly walks by you as he leisurely strolls his territory. We left him gobbling at noon.

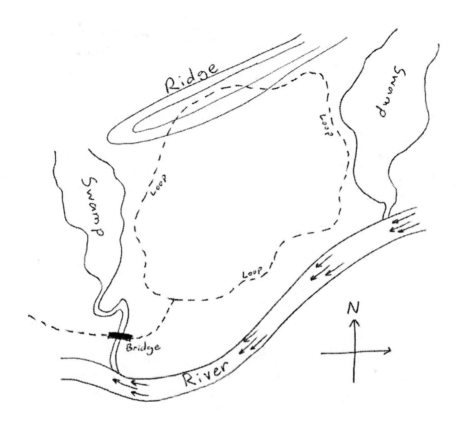

He was nowhere to be found that afternoon, but the next morning, again shortly after ten-o'clock, we made him gobble back where he had that first morning. This time we eased around and up the ridge, moved within eyesight of the swamp, and set up facing westward. He gobbled once during our move and was past the western edge of the ridge where it fell off to meet the swamp on the left and opened up to more open flat, bottomland on the right. We sat among thicker woods atop the point of the ridge, the foliage not yet having progressed as far as the flat land below, with a few dogwoods blooming about. The sky was rich and blue and the air only lightly moving - it was a splendid situation.

He immediately answered our first yelps directly in front of us about 150 yards and gobbled two more times over the next fifteen minutes, the last sounding closer. He shut up and just as enough time elapsed in silence to be concerning, I caught movement out of the corner of my left eye. He had circled us in silence and was sneaking up nearly behind us. My father was to my right, so when he walked behind a tree, I swung my gun and shot as he stepped out at seventeen steps.

I missed.

Missing a turkey is a near sinful act, as we have all done it, but great comfort can be taken if you happen to miss a turkey as well as I did with this one. I missed all of him, did not even knock him down, and before I could get to my feet and take a second shot, he was well out of range flying over the western edge of the swamp. I found no feathers, no blood, and considering the speed and agility with which he flew away, I was assured that he was not wounded and would certainly live to gobble again.

Two mornings later, we indeed found him gobbling at eight-o'clock in a ten-acre wood across the swamp to which he had flown. This tract was even more open than the loop such that you could see 150 yards through the woods easy. We set up against a tree set in the edge of a juvenile bamboo thicket providing great cover. He was at least 200 yards ahead of us. The swamp lay directly at our backs and the event that followed was absolutely astonishing.

It was somewhere around nine-thirty, a full hour and a half into the operation when I fully realized that I was witnessing an event of monumental magnitude. The turkey still sat far out of eyesight, and if he had moved any closer to us, it was not more than fifty yards. It was at that moment that my father leaned over to me and whispered, "Bob, I've counted 335 gobbles so far and I didn't even start counting when we first set up."

We have all told stories of turkeys that gobbled so much as to be ridiculous. Everyone has hunted his own turkey that "gobbled his head off" or "gobbled every minute for a solid hour." I have told plenty of them myself, but this turkey gobbled at a frequency that I could not even imagine possible. He gobbled at our yelps, he gobbled at our clucks, he gobbled at crows, sparrows, and woodpeckers - he gobbled at the wind rustling in the branches above, he gobbled at himself, and he even gobbled at the solemn silence of the forest primeval. If you consider that approximately fifteen minutes of time elapsed from when we set up to when my father started counting, then I would propose that 335 gobbles in a matter of one-hour and fifteen minutes is a hell of a lot more gobbling than ninety-nine percent of all those stories that everyone tells.

The gobbling continued, and just as my father's count crossed 500, we finally caught a glimpse of the turkey still out somewhere near 125 yards. It was approximately ten-o'clock. He was alone and working ever so slowly our direction. By noon, a full four hours into the operation, my father lost count at 1137 gobbles as the turkey moved within fifty yards. He shot the turkey at twelve-twenty.

I have not a mind to try and explain what sort of desires leads an individual to sit and count 1137 gobbles for over four hours. The counter is responsible for answering that vexing question himself.

One might think that sitting at a tree for nearly four and a half hours listening to well over one-thousand gobbles would be fun, but it was not. We honestly considered botching the operation, but it is not easy to leave a gobbling turkey and even harder when you have invested days in pursuit of him. Adding to our predicament, the last two and a half proceeded within eyesight of each other, so if we had left, we would have spooked him, and I am sort of superstitious about doing things like that when you do not have to. So we stuck with it and dealt with all the various problems of sitting in one place for over four hours, such as urges to urinate and body parts going numb.

If you do the math, it took the turkey nearly four and a half hours to move approximately 200 yards, which is just under fifty yards of movement per hour - or just under one yard per minute. Furthermore, he gobbled over 1100 times which comes to roughly four gobbles per minute, or over five gobbles per yard. That is a hell of a lot of gobbling.

I am certain of the fact that my shooting at and missing him two days prior had a strong influence over his extremely cautious pace, but I cannot help but wonder if there was another reason.

I will not claim that turkeys are educated creatures. They do not have book clubs and do not distribute news in papers and magazines. But could it be that they have their own language that only they can interpret - a language inscribed in the woods, both foreign to us and hidden from our eyes. Could it be that he came in so slowly and cautiously because a sign out there at 200 yards forewarned him. Could it be that in his language, he read the very words, "SLOW DEATH AHEAD."

12

THE VANISHING

"But a turkey does have several advantages. He can fly and a man cannot, unaided. His eyesight, especially when it comes to detecting motion, is no less than marvelous, and his hearing simply defies belief. He can hear you yelp at a quarter of a mile, can instantly from that single sound absolutely fix both your direction and your distance, and could if he wanted to, pitch directly from the tree in which he sits and light on your head."

Tom Kelly, *Tenth Legion*

When I think of ways to explain to others the nature of turkeys and why they are so hard to kill, I think of three instances that took place while I was turkey hunting. Coincidentally, all three affairs took place in trees, or with a tree being of central issue. Two of them speak directly of a turkey's senses, and the third, yet totally devoid of turkeys except as a peripheral issue, I use to extrapolate the nature of turkeys and come up with some sort of explanation for the unexplainable. I find it humorous that all three events occurred in trees; all, in some way, demonstrating the improbabilities surrounding turkey hunting.

All my life I have tried to explain to others who do not hunt any game at all, including those who shoot deer, just how serious a barricade the sensory talents of a turkey are to calling and killing one.

I mean not to belittle deer hunting, as it can be valid if approached in the right manner. But too often deer hunters crawl in stands and shoot deer and effectively change the name of their pursuit from deer hunting to deer shooting. After all, most people properly call the social gathering of hunters for the purpose of killing dove a dove shoot. We sometimes call it dove hunting, but in actuality it is dove shooting. There is no hunting involved, unless if you consider searching for your spot on the field as hunting. In that case, it really is spot hunting/dove shooting. You sit and shoot. You do not hunt.

And being in similarity to dove shooting, the more deer you have the more closely the sport resembles pure unadulterated shooting and not hunting.

I cannot be blamed for the supremacy attitude turkey hunters feel over deer hunters. Such attitudes extend far back into the literature, as nearly a whole chapter in *Tenth Legion* is devoted to explaining why.

But deer hunting in the South today is far removed from the gutless deer drives Tom Kelly so eloquently described in 1970. It is now a far more respectable sport, and if not for the portion who still guzzle beer and sip on bourbon until one in the morning, head out at nine AM and return at ten-thirty, it could be considered legitimate. The few who pursue deer properly get a bad wrap.

I say all this knowing some of my friends who hunt deer in Clay County may be offended by this kind of speak. After all, they may just end up reading this very book. Someone will undoubtedly inform them of my mentions of them in print, and nobody is going to turn away an opportunity to read of his own fame and stardom.

But theirs much more closely resembles deer hunting like it ought to be than deer shooting, although that too can depend upon the person of whom we are speaking.

The deer in Clay County are big and few, and require an element of woodsmanship in locating game movements and maybe a foundation of knowledge of climatic influences upon game behaviors to kill a big buck yearly. If they have demonstrated such skills in the taking of a buck, then surely they can rightfully claim to have hunted and killed it.

On the other hand, there are those who climb into fifteen-foot shooting houses built by hired hand, complete with steps, doors, locks, carpet, and moveable padded benches inside, calling it exactly what it is, a shooting house, and in an irony full of humor, claim to be deer hunting. It just is not so.

Neither of these two forms of hunting or pseudohunting or shooting (depending on which method you are referring or who is conducting the affair) really appeals to me, although shooting a deer out of a warm carpeted house is a much better way to pass time than sitting cold in a deer stand and seeing nothing.

Even with this deer shooting, I have no problem. I enjoy shooting dove immensely, even if it is not true hunting, and find no fault at all if you enjoy deer shooting. Just call it what it is.

Since I do so much hunting of feathered creatures, I neither have the time to shoot deer, nor the patience, since accumulating upwards of twenty half days or more in silence, and cold for that matter, is required before finally pulling the trigger on a buck. I can spend upwards of twenty half days hunting turkeys and will be surrounded by all kind of noises, turkey noises mostly, and whether or not I kill a turkey, I will enjoy the whole affair. Plus it is a little warmer.

And now it seems ironic to me, that I use situations that occurred in trees to explain the nature of turkeys, when deer hunters, who spend so much time in trees, ought really to be the authority on the subject. I will try.

One typical Spring day, my father and I heard a turkey gobble at daybreak across a creek below a ridge that we often listened from. We had hunted this land enough to know three important characteristics of the creek. First, the vegetation around it was a thick mess, not with briars, but with scrubby bushes and trees of unknown species to me, making it difficult to get through. Second, if we were to make it through the brush, the creek would be deep enough and wide enough to prevent any kind of semi-dry passage. Third, if we elected to swim across, the other side would present three-year-old cutover with half-inch diameter briars to sit and put our backs up against, and the turkey would have to be called within five feet to permit proper identification. So, in going against steadfast rules, we elected to set up on the ridge we were on, about half way down, and on the wrong side of the creek from this turkey. It was from there we called.

It was a typical exchange of words. The turkey gobbled well and around six-thirty, roughly thirty minutes after the whole affair began, he left his roost and flew to us. We first spotted him somewhere around fifty feet above the creek bottom gliding directly to our point on the ridge. The closer he got, the more I realized he was actually flying in a direct line for us. Seventy yards, fifty, forty - it was if he was intending to land right in front of us. Thirty yards, twenty, ten - he pulled his wings up, flapped once to gain a little height, and lit not fifteen feet above me in a limb off the very tree I had my back against.

Let me take up issue here with two points. First, one of my rules is not to shoot turkeys in the air unless I have first missed them on the ground. It is not wrong or against the law, but is a bit less honorable, especially if the turkey was never called up to begin with. Truthfully, I worry about wounding a turkey more than anything. I could have shot that turkey when he was twenty feet high and ten yards out, easy, as I do floater doves, and talk today about the length of his beard or the color of his feathers. But I did not. I neither look down upon nor try to discourage others from shooting turkeys out of the air, though I can comparatively say all mine were killed the right way, by calling them up on the ground.

Of second point in issue is the confirming of the descriptions we hear all the time about the incredible ability of a turkey to hear so well. I can say these tales are 100 percent accurate because this is exactly what happened to me, though the turkey chose a much more comfortable place to stand than my head. To further state my case, it was I who was doing the calling, and the turkey lit over my head and not my father who sat ten yards to my left.

I never did see that turkey sitting in the limb above me, but learned quite a lot from just listening to him. He was too directly overhead for me to twist my body backwards and sideways while simultaneously cocking my head over and up underneath to be able to see him. I tried to do so, but could not without moving my body, which I was afraid he would see. My father could see him and watched him nearly the whole time strutting up and down that limb for nearly fifteen minutes. He gobbled six or seven times and did a lot of drumming.

I doubt there are many men who have experienced being that close to a genuine wild turkey gobbler for as long as my father and I did that morning. As such, I doubt there are many men who have been that close to real gobbling or drumming.

We pride ourselves in the South of having the best turkeys and claim their superiority to other species, or at least I do, although they may not be much better than an *Osceola*. Honest to God wild turkeys as we have here in Alabama, gobble loud enough to scare the hell out of you when you are very close to one. Their gobble hits you quick, like of clap of thunder, and resonates deep, and sounds nothing like a barnyard turkey to the lay person. In fact, they sound much different than the gobbles from the western turkeys I have heard on the television hunting shows (Merriams and Rio Grandes are fabulous species to film because they come in so easy - often whole groups of gobblers come running in together). Lovett E. Williams, Jr. detailed this for us in his writings.

The present day domesticated turkey is a descendant of the *Mealagris gallapovo gallapovo*, or Gould's turkey of Mexico, and was originally domesticated some two-thousand years ago by the ancestors of cultures including Mimbres, Anasazi, Inca and Mayan. Spaniards exported them around 1500 A.D. where they spread throughout Europe and eventually returned on ships back to the Americas.

Oddly, though the domesticated turkey is a direct descendant of the Gould's, Williams notes that the gobble of the *Mealagris gallapovo merriami* (the Merriam) more closely resembles the gobble of the domesticated turkey than any other wild species.

Current thoughts hold that the Merriam turkey was brought to the Southwestern United States from Mexico by the ancient Pueblo Indians and in some manner became wild following. Speculation consists of three theories. They either escaped the Pueblos; they were allowed to roam free, or they were simply abandoned. I have never hunted turkeys out West. For that matter, I have never hunted turkeys in any state other than Alabama. But what this information confirms to me is that I have no desire to hunt turkeys out West because they are not anything like the turkeys we have in the Southeast. They are too close to domestic.

My father tells me he could have easily killed that turkey sitting in the tree by shouldering his gun when the turkey turned his back to him with his tail feathers up. But he had the same foolhardy delusion as I had. We both knew that in a matter of moments, that turkey would pitch down to the ground right in front of us, not more than thirty yards, and let us (or me) shoot him. But the turkey never did, and after thirty minutes of strutting and drumming and gobbling up and down the limb, he picked up and flew back to where he had come from. It was over. He never did come back.

The next affair took place in a tree also, though this time I was able to see the whole situation into which I had fallen.

I started down the dirt road away from my truck through four or five-year-old cut over, just beginning to get fairly thick with overgrowth. It was good and dark, as yet the sun was only cracking the horizon of the eastern sky. Not a breath of wind was to be felt, just as I like it.

Approaching the woods line, roughly twenty yards in front, I felt the deep sound of a drum, as drumming so often is only felt anyway. The sensation was convincing enough to stop me in my tracks. I waited a brief moment, and after I felt it again, I positively certain it was drumming. Since drumming is so often only felt and not heard, it can be difficult at times to fix its location, as was the case in this situation. Since I had no confidence as to this turkey's location, I preceded no further. Spooking a gobbler was not something I had intended less than ten minutes from the truck before daylight. I had to find a place somewhere among the thorny brush overtaking the four or five-year-old clear-cut to sit.

By now the eastern sky was providing just enough light to be able to make out silhouettes of objects such as trees or half trees in the dark, and to my left, five feet within the briars, was just such a half tree, broken off some fifteen feet high. I slipped through the briars, though if you were listening you might swear the briars attacked me, and was delighted to find a decent seat with the base wide enough to do some good at breaking my silhouette and some room in front to maneuver my gun. I faced the woods.

The dirt road, now at my right, continued straight towards the woods, and penetrated the woods line perpendicular for 100 yards. From the continued drumming, I supposed the turkey was roosted somewhere near the road and probably fifty to seventy-five yards within the woods.

The sky grew brighter, the drumming continued, and I became even more pleasantly surprised to find my visibility through the briars was well down the road and into the woods a good thirty yards. I slipped my gloves and head net on, and reasoned this was as good a place as any to call up a turkey.

I sat and listened and watched the eastern sky invade the western sky. It grew brighter until the red birds began to sing. Then an owl hooted in the distance, and what followed was not a clap of thunder, but a clap of gobble, so loud and so close, that it scared the hell out of me. I screamed, honestly, albeit softly and likely inaudible over the gobble, but a real scream. Twenty degrees left, maybe thirty yards away, and on the edge of the woods, in a thin, twisted, tree of sorts, sat a gobbler. It took no less than two seconds to know this was not the turkey that I originally heard drumming. First of all, he was far too close, and second, he was in wrong direction. Third, by gobbling, he sent his thin roost limb in extreme motion, bouncing up and down and all around nearly tossing him off. This was not a limb in which a gobbler could manage to strut and drum. This was a second turkey, and much closer. In fact, close enough to shoot.

He would gobble, the other would drum, and I sat motionless watching and listening to it all. But as the sun continued to light the sky, my fate was sealed. With all my camouflage and gloves and head net on, but one part of my body was exposed - my eyes, and it became apparent that with each blink of my eyes, he would wheel his long neck around and study me over, again and again.

I need not go into the happenings that followed. I did not kill the turkey, either of them - Ok? Let us just say the sky got a little too bright for me to stay hidden and be done with it. But mind you, I could have killed him, as it had initially been dark enough for me to possibly shoulder my gun undetected. But I did not, because I have rules as to only shoot turkeys that I have called up. I neither look down upon nor try to discourage others from shooting turkeys they did not call, though I can comparatively say all mine were killed the right way, by calling them up - except for the time...

The last affair took place in a tree, also, but only involved turkeys as a peripheral issue. It was a crisp Fall day, and my father and I had topped a mountain in Clay County. The sun had risen, and after a half-hearted chase of some distant yelping, we eased out to the end of a ridge and sat down. At this point, we were no closer to turkeys than when we had started. But the sun was warming our bodies, the air was still, and we were delighted to sit back and soak it all in. We sat there, a good half hour, whispering amongst ourselves.

Times like these, when some of the seriousness and focus is absent from the hunt, are great times for watching and enjoying other animals, like squirrels. One just happened to appear before us.

It started out foregoing among the thick and dry mat of leaves on the ground. Rain had ceased for a month, and the humidity was low enabling this squirrel to make an awful lot of noise in the brittle leaves. He scurried about, poking and prodding his head through the leaves in search of oak and hickory acorns. Up on a log and off the log; up on a stump and off the stump. His playfulness left us feeling just giddy. Then up a tree he went, not twenty yards in front of us, and silence reigned again.

He continued up this tree until he reached the first limb some fifty feet up and scampered out to its end. There, he sat down, much as a dog sits, and looked about as if contemplating a jump. Looking around, I too contemplated his jumping.

I fully understand that squirrels are acrobats in trees, and can jump farther than you ever anticipate and grab a hold of the thinnest of twigs. In this particular case, however, there were no trees, let alone twigs, anywhere near this squirrel for him to jump to. For whatever reason, the twenty yards in all 180 degrees of which he had to choose, was open, without any thing growing. So I too contemplated his jumping, and wondered what in the hell he would jump to.

Then, in a manner that made me want to jump up and yell and scream in hopes of scaring some sense into him, he jumped, before I could, and near missed any trees by a good fifty squirrel lengths. He hit the ground hard, just on the other side of a fallen log, not ten yards away, with a dampening "thug"—it was not even close.

I make light of it now, but at the time, the whole event transpired as if in slow motion before my eyes. It just seemed to me that, for whatever reason, this squirrel was jumping to his death, on purpose. Suicide? I know squirrels are acrobats, and can handle all sorts of falls and mis-jumps and can live to tell about them, but this was a serious jump, of great heights, at least far higher than I would think even a squirrel would be able to survive. The dampening thug we heard was confirming enough. Suicide it was! I had never heard of suicide in nature and wondered what sort of family affairs a rodent must be dealing with to commit such a crime. Honestly, my father and I discussed its very possibility and then erupted in big ball of laughter over the whole incident.

We sat and watched, and never saw that squirrel again, nor did we ever hear it again. We even got up and thoroughly explored the whole area in which he landed, but he was nowhere to be found. It seemed impossible! He did not run off because we did not hear him run off, and if he had done so, we would have undoubtedly heard him as he would have made an unavoidable loud racket through the dry, brittle leaves on the forest floor. And he did not scamper away up a tree, silently, because he would have had to cross some twenty yards of forest floor to get to a tree, and that puts us back to not hearing him again. Umm!

Which brings me to my last point. Apparently squirrels have a supernatural ability I once thought only turkeys possessed. It is an ability not yet explored by scientists but witnessed by many a turkey hunter. It is an ability I cannot explain myself but can in all seriousness attest to its occurrence—the supernatural ability to disappear into thin air. It is all I have to explain how turkeys can slip behind a tree at forty yards and not appear on the other side. It is all I have to explain the stories of turkeys shot at thirty yards, even watched fall, but never found or seen running off or flying away.

So it happens with turkeys, and by revelation I had found it happened to squirrels. I suppose by extrapolation that all animals can do it, if they wished to, although turkeys just make use of it whole lot more.

I wish not to belabor the point.

13

A LESS THAN OBVIOUS CONNECTION

"Most of this book, up to this point, covers my first thirty-three years. The era of Gabe Meadow, Kyle Delk, and Tony McCleb. The era of classical woods-hunting of gobbling turkeys in the Springtime. Without a doubt this is the most challenging way to hunt turkeys."

Gene Nunnery, *The Old Pro Turkey Hunter*

Buried deep in the pages of *Tenth Legion*, I have been drawn to one distinct and all encompassing thought expressed by Tom Kelly. It is a bold statement that is nearly impossible to be accepted by any other than a true turkey hunter, a member of the Tenth Legion. Believe me when I say that I have tried several times, with many a non-turkey hunter, using all forms of logic and reasoning I possess and invariably have failed every time. It is a near futile exercise, but let me try anyway.

Kelly says, "He [a turkey hunter] will operate primarily in a climate not of desire but of compulsion. This is painfully evident in my own case. I do not hunt turkeys because I want to. I hunt them because I have to. I would really rather not do it, but I am helpless in the grip of my compulsion."

Take a hypothetical Spring day of any given Spring season, say April 5th, when the tender young leaves ought to be sprouting and the dogwoods blooming, adding splendor to the woods. For argument's sake, lets make it a Friday whose morning was a day God created for turkey hunting. And lets say you are a turkey hunter, a member of the Legion, and you had the good fortune of escaping civilization that morning, whether it was before work or school or simply during some time off and had gone hunting. You worked one under the rich blue sky, in the breathless air, among the pristine sounds of nature for two hours. He gobbled well, answered your yelps like he ought to, and even came close enough once that you could clearly make out the under-drumming in his gobble. You maneuvered, changed tactics a time or two, tried different yelpers, different calls, even played the silent game, but when it all ended, you were thoroughly defeated.

Now, later in the day you find yourself back in your routine place in society, confined by walls and surrounded by people who have no connection with the outdoors or hunting for that matter - some not even aware that turkeys exist in the wild, nor that God in his infinite creativity placed turkeys in the wild for the specific purpose of being hunted, and that he created gobbles solely to stimulate members of the Legion. But your coworkers or classmates do not know this. They do not know that while they slept, you rose early under darkness and headed outdoors before the sun even rose -or while they were showering, you had been working one for an hour. They do not know your troubles.

85

But you do have troubles, like being held captive to your thoughts and imaginations -held captive back in the woods from where you started the day. There will be so many different situations and visions and wonders and what ifs that you will dwell on. You will endlessly ponder what he looked like. Were his legs long? How big was he? Was his head a glowing blue or a deep fiery red? Did he have other turkeys with him and if so, is that why you could not bring him in? Through your mind, over and over you will consider the consequences of different tactics if you had chosen them instead, such as setting up on a different ridge, yelping less, or if you had shooed away that hen you saw heading his direction. And all the while you will understand the peace that you had that morning away from it all, alone, doing what so few are willing to do.

These thoughts eventually become interlaced with and then give way to new thoughts of tomorrow, your second chance. You further ponder your strategy - whether you should listen at a different spot, how you will handle situations differently if he acts similar to today, what you can do if he acts different, or worst of all, if he does not gobble.

And you will look about and see people, coworkers, classmates, and friends, all of whom are free of this burden that so afflicts you. You see the freedom in their steps and their deliverance to which they are ignorant. They act as you really ought to act, as most normal people act on Fridays, by consuming their thoughts with upcoming weekend activities, family get togethers, yard work, golf, and lazy weekend trips. It is inevitable, that after watching their innocent steps of simplicity day after day, you eventually are inundated with yet another emotion - envy.

So why do we turkey hunters continue our pursuit? The answer requires a long and exhaustive introspection to reason through our innate desires. I am not referring to the thrill we all feel when we hear a gobble or all that heart-pounding stuff that occurs when seeing a turkey stand at a distance of thirty yards. We all enjoy those aspects, and most of us will claim that experiencing them keeps us coming back. I am not trying to devalue the importance of gobbling, as it is without question the most unique and defining aspect of real wild turkey hunting. Edward A. McIlhenny noted this in *The Wild Turkey and Its Hunting.* "Take away the delight of the gobbling season from the turkey hunter, and the quest of the wild turkey would lose its fascination." Gene Nunnery agrees in *The Old Pro Turkey Hunter*, saying, "The two main things a turkey gobbler does that fascinates a hunter is his gobbling and strutting. Normally he does a lot of both. A turkey's gobbling and strutting are his trademark. I don't recall reading even one of the many good turkey stories that doesn't stress the gobbling of the turkeys." But if gobbling and strutting was all there was to it, we could leave our guns at home and be just as satisfied. I think that there is a combination of so many variables involved that it may not be possible to put down in words our reasons. Instead, it must be experienced to be understood.

I have thought long and hard concerning my own desires, and I hope I may be able to at least reveal the tip of the iceberg to you. Be patient and take this a little slow. Things are about to get thick and heavy.

Merrian-Webster's Collegiate Dictionary defines transcendentalism as, "a philosophy that asserts the primacy of the spiritual and the transcendental over the material and empirical." I define it as a pretentious way of thinking for those too selfish and intellectually inclined to associate comfortably with the rest of us ignorant-minded people participating in what is they think is the blind leading the blind. To the Emersons, Alcots, Fullers and Parkers of both past and present, this applies, and no doubt there will be some in the future too.

But one of them, Henry David Thoreau, likewise afflicted with the burden of his own intellect, I have discovered a connection in thought, all be it very slight. I wish not to propose a commonality in belief that the physical world is a mere reflection of our inner spiritual world, or that the modern advances in society only serve to enslave us further rather than to free our burden. But Thoreau's most well know work, *Walden*, written in 1850, illustrates one man's view of a hierarchal appreciation of nature and speaks tangentially of my own perspective. Am I as snobbish as they?

The transcendentalists did argue for nature as God's creation to be revered, and that one's actions in dealing with it, whether using it directly or indirectly, affected one's level of reverence.

For two years, Thoreau escaped the civilization of Concord to live among the scenic beauty of Walden Pond, under the law of his own effort. His meager existence afforded him maximum communion with the nature that surrounded him, finding the greatest fulfillment by appreciation of its beauty; becoming truly alive while the people of the village were perpetually asleep.

I have no quarrel with the conclusion that Thoreau in fact experienced a deep bonding and respect for the land and animals of Walden Pond, likely far greater than most today as well as those whom he left at the village. To live meagerly, depending wholly on the land, and to have enough leisure time to do absolutely nothing but observe the surroundings in a setting as gorgeous as Walden Pond would enlighten most anybody. To depend wholly on the land changes one's viewpoint. Thoreau repetitively emphasizes his opinion that man is part of nature, not above it, and that if man can learn to live off it and depend upon it, then he can find truth and meaning in his existence.

If you can cut through all this purist bull crap, maybe you will see that these two suppositions are flawed. First, nature is not divine, and second, man is not a part of nature. This incongruent thinking is pure hogwash that assigns a higher-ranking status to nature that simply is not true or justified. Nature was set into motion by the true divinity, God, and perpetuates in beauty that is worthy of appreciation because the laws that it follows were laid out perfectly and wonderfully by God. Nature knows neither of its own beauty nor of its own existence. It is not an independent thinker. And contrary to the thinking of the modern day environmentalist movement, mankind is better than and distinctly separate from and above the land and plants and the beasts that together compromise what we call nature. God said it himself in Genesis, "Let us make man in our image, in our likeness, and let them rule over the fish of the sea sand the birds of the air..."

But the naturalist who views hunting as sinful is blinded to this truth and will claim a greater appreciation and reverence for nature than the rest of us ignorant-minded bloody barbarians that kill its beast for sport. For those hypocrites who live in the Hollywood hills of California, in multimillion-dollar homes, and intermittently retire to luxurious resorts or homes in the wilderness to commune with nature and claim a superior attitude towards the character of nature, no effort shall be wasted. But for the fewer individuals who have dropped off the deep end so to speak, such as those who live in the tops of trees for two years continuously, which is far more respectable than anything the Hollywood stars do, an argument is in order.

In 1927, an Einstein sort of person published a paper containing the following statement, "the more precisely the position is determined, the less precisely the momentum is known in this instant and vice versa." The gentleman's name was Heisenberg and the statement eloquently explained in his paper is known as the Heisenberg Uncertainty Principle. What it explains is that when dealing with elementary particles in quantum mechanics, the physical act of measuring one aspect of the particle, such as its position, requires a trade off in the accuracy of measuring another, such as momentum. The more precise the measurement in one of these quantities becomes, the less certain the measurement of the other becomes.

A serious discussion of quantum mechanics is far from the scope of this paper, not that I am all that qualified to lead it anyhow, but this principle can be successfully applied to all sorts of various aspects in our world, both the quantum mechanical kind and those a bit more tangible.

The problem with the naturalist way of thinking is that you cannot have both the pristine, undisturbed, primeval forest and the enjoyment of experiencing it at the same time. The more of one you have the less of the other is available. The primeval forest can only exist purely if it remains undisturbed by those who wish to enjoy it. Their presence alone disrupts the equilibrium, and those who wish most to leave nature to exist under its own influence can only enjoy it by disrupting this equilibrium they long for. Because man is not a part of nature, contrary to those who agree with Thoreau, nature fears man, and its animals have a tendency to do things like run away from and avoid humans when their presence is detected. So the more one tries to experience the nature, the more nature avoids their presence such that that which they seek escapes them and is no longer what they truly wish for. The primeval forest can only be enjoyed if you are in it, and since we humankind are not able to do things like become invisible, we are detected and the creatures flee from our presence. You cannot be wholly in and wholly enjoy the primeval state at the same time. One must give to the other.

The primeval state can exist perfectly if you are not there to disturb it, but if you are not there, then how can you enjoy it? And one can attempt to fully explore and enjoy the primeval by being in it and walking among it and standing in it, but this changes it from the primeval such that the enjoyment one experiences is not truly of what is sought. The primeval has given way to your enjoyment. The more precise one's enjoyment of nature is experienced, the less precisely the undisturbed primeval is known and vice versa.

But what if you were to become a part of nature, as Thoreau put it, but in a different sort of way? Instead of falsely elevating nature beyond what it is, or belittling mankind, what if you use your supremacy to masquerade yourself as a part of or become one entity with the primeval, and manipulate it within its very own set of laws, such that although your presence if fully known to the primeval, it is fooled and thinks you are one of it? In this way, the principle can be broken and both the enjoyment of and the existence of the primeval state can both exist fully at the same time.

Is that not what we turkey hunters do? We manipulate turkeys in their own environment, the primeval forest, within their own set of laws, such that we become a part of their existence. We hide with camouflage and use their language and become thoroughly involved in their world, such that it accepts us as one of its own. Because we are able to do this, we are able to more fully enjoy this part of nature than any casual stroller or bird watcher or photographer. Even Gene Nunnery agrees, saying, "I know a lot of people enjoy bird watching. None of them could even come close to the joy I get out of turkeys watching."

And I can enjoy wild turkeys and any Southern woods or forest far greater than they too, which all leads to a greater appreciation and admiration. No naturalist or animal rights activist can appreciate the looks and behavior and domain of a wild turkey more than I.

For many of you, the same is true, except for those of you who shamefully set up over decoys on the edges of fields. Decoys are for ducks, not turkeys. Thank God the great state of Alabama still recognizes this fact and has not yet allowed their use. Every other state in the union with the exception of New Hampshire has lost its own dignity - and who the hell would have ever expected Alabama and New Hampshire to see eye to eye on an issue such as hunting.

My primary objection to the use of decoys for hunting turkeys is two fold. Decoys entice hunters to set up on the edges of green fields and pastures and discourages them from moving from situations when they ought to. Second, when that old turkey does come on in, his attention will be focused on the decoy and not the hunter, which brings a level of comfort to the game that ought not to be there. All this effectively turns a turkey hunt into a turkey shoot, which can be highly successful but looses a sense of respect. It takes much of the tactic away that makes turkey hunting what it is.

If you hunt turkeys long enough and try to do it properly, your going to develop your own set of idiosyncrasies in regard to what is proper and what is not. And whether or not hunting turkeys in fields becomes a part of your own set of do's and don'ts, I can tell you that killing a turkey in the middle of a woods is infinitely more enjoyable than if you kill one in a field, even if decoys are never part of the equation. To have an old turkey gobble and drum and move around seventy-five yards in front of you without your being able to see him or only catching occasional glimpses, all the while being connected only through sound, and if he should do this for an hour or two, will absolutely engross every bit of you that there is. And if he should then come on in, slowly, interrupting his stroll every three feet to stand tall and peer around every tree and look with every bit of attention he has for you, and knowing that whereas a man can see the second hand of a clock moving, a turkey can see the hour hand moving, your soul will be absolutely ripped to shreds. And if you should know him, having battled him many times prior, loosing each time, you can square rather than multiply this emotion.

You see, turkey hunting the way it ought to be done allows you to experience a great emotional paradox. In one sense, when you make one gobble, you sit by a tree and wish beyond all hope that he would immediately come marching in, the faster the better. You sit there and hope that he gobbles every ten seconds, thus allowing you to know which way he is coming. And once you do see him coming through the woods, if he never stops and stands tall and thoroughly looks you over, then comfort will nearly become you. And when you set out from your truck, you hope it is not 100 yards down the road when all this occurs, and if you are really lucky, he trips over a log and breaks his neck running in at forty-five yards so you do not have to waist shell killing him too.

But in another sense, during those melodramatic moments where he is gobbling just out of sight at eighty yards, or when you can hear him walking and drumming for thirty minutes but you cannot see him, the other side of you is tugging with the subconscious appreciation of the torture that damn turkey is putting you through. This all results in an awesome mixing of opposite emotions, and can only occur if you hunt turkeys in the middle of woods, not fields.

In *Tenth Legion*, Tom Kelly goes on to say, "In all your dealings with turkeys, the most valuable piece of equipment that you have is your ear, and the most used of your senses is your sense of sound. Your sense of hearing is so far superior to your sense of sight in this respect that I do really believe a blind man could kill more turkeys than a deaf man. You will hear infinitely more turkeys than you will ever see."

It should be plainly evident to us all that Tom Kelly wrote those words in a different era. He wrote it back when hunting turkeys in the woods was the norm, when you really had to work to find and kill turkeys, and it was in this method that all those legendary stories occurred.

I am not saying I will never again kill a turkey in a field. I have done so in the past and most likely will again - and I will relish in the victory too. But I will not ever set up before the crack of dawn one the edge of one and sit there staring at an empty field while one is gobbling elsewhere off in the distance. And when I do kill one in a field, it will not be done so overlooking a set of decoys spread at twenty yards, even if the state of Alabama allows their use. But for those I do kill in a field, even if I chased them and hunted them around for the better part of the morning finally ending up on the edge of a field, I can guarantee the memory they will create will not match the ones that occur in the woods.

Woods hunting, which is where the true wild turkey domain occurs (for the South anyhow), lets you experience a slice of the primeval forest—an experience so many of us relish. It is that feeling of being away from it all, intimate with nature, connecting with one of its most glorious creatures mostly by sound, occasionally by sight, amongst a myriad of sounds in a Springtime forest—the echoing hammer of a woodpecker down in a hollow, a squirrel barking on the next ridge, cardinals filling the still dawn air with a confluence of singing, the desolate whoosh of wind through the tree tops—and a backdrop of variegated green leaves budding from the trees with a scattering of white dogwood blossoms all around is nothing short of inspirational.

It is for these reasons collectively; becoming a part of the undisturbed setting described above, with an overpowering obsession to kill a turkey, and the unfading, rewarding feeling when doing so, that I am a turkey hunter.

Maybe now, even if only very slight, some of you understand.

14

CHANGES

"Looking back over the fifty-three years, I find a vast difference in turkey hunting, old style and new style. In deciding at what point the great change came, I have concluded it occurred about twenty years ago."

Gene Nunnery, *The Old Pro Turkey Hunter*

Turkey hunting in this day and age has changed quite a bit since I was born. That statement coming forth from the mouth of a twenty-three-year-old might raise the hair on the back of some of your necks. And you are fully justified. I cannot even begin to comprehend the changes that have occurred through the years for those of you who have been after wild turkeys for twice as long as I am old. And I am not going to attempt to do so. There has been plenty of literature published about the near extinction and successful restocking of turkeys that took place during the first three quarters of this century. It is a remarkable subject and quite important, in my opinion, for every turkey hunter to be educated on such matters.

I am grateful too. No I will not be able to sit with my grandchildren gathered around and talk of economic depressions, walking barefoot to and from school, uphill both ways, in the snow, nor of the rarity of turkeys, and even more so, of the rarity of killing one. Mine will be less heroic, just as ancient, and all directed towards stirring little children's emotions about the ease in which they live.

I will talk of different tales, for instance of when my father and I split fifty-thousand acres of national forest land with few others back in the 70's and 80's. We were turkey hunters, a breed that nearly suffered the same extinction threats as the turkeys did in the 30's and 40's. But in the late 80's, as the growth of turkey populations took off, turkey hunter populations rose too.

About five years ago on opening day of turkey season, I found myself in this same national forest I grew up turkey hunting. The few weeks prior, I had toured the property a couple of times to refresh my memory as to the lay of the land and to familiarize my self as to which sections of woods remained, which sections were now gone, and which sections had emerged into huntable growth during the previous decade.

I found that for the most part, the forest looked pretty much the same. After all, woods always do look like woods. But I was surprised to find the complexity and intricacy of roads that had been cut through and of the progress the loggers had made in clearing the land. I accepted the changes, for what else could I do, as the roads make for easier hunting, and although there was a little less huntable terrain, the whole operation seemed as though it should thoroughly suffice—until I showed opening morning.

As I drove to my predestined spot, I found a multitude of vehicles parked in every side road, nook and cranny one could possibly back a truck into. I had to check my watch to make sure I had not mistakenly chosen the wrong date to go turkey hunting and, instead, shown up for the Burr & Forman Dove shoot on opening day of dove season. To tell you the truth, I could hardly find a place to park in the fifty-thousand acres, let alone hunt in my predestined spot. I finally settled for an area that looked like it held about as many turkeys as the Grand Canyon, and by ten-o'clock that morning, I was fancying the idea of actually being in the grand Canyon instead of this wasteland. The Grand Canyon would have at least given me something aesthetically pleasing to sit and stare and marvel at.

It is just a fact that I am going to have to get used to, though I probably never will. Increasing turkey populations ultimately lead to greater populations of those who wish to shoot them, and there is nothing I can do about it. However, there is no legitimacy in implicating the numbers as long as you are one of them. I am no more likely to quit to help out the situation than the next guy.

But I do sense that something has happened to turkey hunting between the times of my youth in the old national forest and today that makes it a little different, and I do not like it. I guess I can sum up what this something is that I do not like by saying that turkey hunting has become too commercialized.

What are the rewards today's generation of turkey hunter seeks? I dare say, that while the crusades to promote turkey hunting and make it more available to everyone have been successful, an element of what turkey hunting used to be, and what it should be, has been lost. Advanced knowledge and reformed tactics have made turkey hunting easier, both for the experienced and rookies. And that is good. But it has also perverted the motives of hunters as they enter the woods today from the noble pursuits of the days of old.

A turkey hunter should not enter the woods to kill a turkey, for with this objective, critical ingredients to the turkey hunting experience are lost. A turkey hunter should enter to do battle with a turkey, with all intentions and tactics of winning that battle. There is a difference.

In the old days (for me that means in the late 70's or early 80's), every turkey hunter wore the same camouflage, yelped with the same tone and frequency as Ben Lee did on his audio tapes, and used shotguns that were no more made for shooting turkeys than for shooting deer, duck or whatever creature you pleased. Now, camouflage and calls and turkey shotguns are big business. Many would attest that the whole infiltration is supremely better. I say equivocal on the matter.

I personally believe the old World War II army print is as good a camouflage as any camouflage you can find on the market today, if not better. You know the old pattern I am talking about. It has a beige background with irregular blobs of green and brown scattered about, as if placed by a two-inch paintbrush. If you have a copy of the *Tenth Legion* published in the 70's by Spur Enterprises or the *Old Pro Turkey Hunter* by Gene Nunnery, look on the back covers and you will find photos of Tom Kelly or Ben Rogers Lee or Jack Dudley dressed in such attire. Find me this upcoming Spring and you too, will find me dressed in such attire. I believe in it so firmly, that I seek out and buy any of the ancient stuff I can find, whether it be in flea markets or old surplus stores. The way I figure, they are not making the stuff anymore, so I had better stock up on all I can now.

Shotguns have also been remodeled to conform to the new turkey hunter's requests. They are now factory camouflaged, which is fine by me, though it probably does not make a bit of difference. Barrels are cut way shorter now allowing you to nestle in tighter places and swing your gun more freely; and chokes are designed to deliver the tightest of patterns. Couple these ultra-tight patterns with the shorter barrels, and you nearly have a handgun to shoot, or with the accuracy of such.

Remembering the geometric rules we all learned in high school, congruent triangles share dimensions of equal proportion to one another. Since I am not all that steady when I am shooting a turkey, it is likely the bead on the end of the barrel is not perfectly centered over the receiver and may be off a millimeter or two or three. For each millimeter or two or three off, the pattern at thirty yards is going to be off center by a proportion of the distance to the turkey to the length of the barrel multiplied by this millimeter or two or three. To make this French simple, if the barrel is one-yard long and the bead is one-millimeter off center the receiver, then the center of the pattern is going to be off by 30 x 1 millimeter, or 30 millimeters at thirty yards. Thirty millimeters is three centimeters, which is not that much, but barrels are shorter than one-yard in length, and a 20" barrel, or just over half a yard, will give a pattern off center by nearly ten centimeters at thirty yards if the bead is off center by two millimeters, and if you just simply aim off by up to five inches to begin with, which is fully possible and highly likely, a five or six-inch or even ten-inch pattern is not going to be wide enough to hit the turkey effectively. Instead, you will miss. It only takes one shot (pellet) to crack the vertebral column in the neck or penetrate the skull to render a turkey unable to fly or run away, leaving them like we always see them, flopping, so there is not any need to have a pattern ninety percent dense in a five-inch circle at thirty yards anyway. I think these two reasons explain, or at least contribute to, all the turkeys we hear of being missed these days.

In compensation, you can have a shotgun with sights or fitted with a scope, but in my opinion, these have no place in turkey hunting circles, as their rights belong to deer hunters. First of all, they look silly on a shotgun. But also, I believe a weapon with an ultra-tight pattern, chambered with 3 ½" magnum shells, and having some sort of sighting device entices hunters to take shots at too far a distance. Not only do I not want to look down a shotgun and see sights, but I also do not understand how you are supposed to shoot a turkey running away or flying away after you have missed him if you have sights or a scope on your shotgun.

As for modern turkey calls, I give - hands down. They are far superior today, and our knowledge base of turkeys and the calls they make are far better known today. But in a way, this lack of knowledge in the old days led to more mystery and talk surrounding turkeys and their behavior that was just plain fun. We did not know about cutting and fighting calls or even the wide variance of locator falls you see on the market today. We had six calls in our vocabulary - the cluck, yelp, cackle, kee-kee-run, owl, crow call, and that is it, just like Ben Lee did it.

Now matters are quite different. Have you picked up a magazine recently to read a turkey hunting article? They tell you how to call and when to call and how to pattern turkeys, when in truth, turkeys pattern very poorly.

Now even though I am only twenty-three, I have been hunting turkeys longer than many hunters in the woods these days, and with all the turkeys I have heard gobble, I do not believe I have ever heard a "booming gobble" loud enough to "rattle the forest floor" below. But I read about such turkeys in these articles. They have "thundering" gobbles and "ultrasonic" drums that sound like jets breaking the sound barrier. They are commonly described as being long-beards, bronze barons, monarchs of the forest, or iridescent ghosts.

Maybe it is just a personal disliking for these descriptions, and I really have no rightful place in criticizing them. But I feel that there is a right and wrong way in referring to turkeys and turkey hunting. If you read the legendary old tales or are fortunate enough to acquaint yourself with one of those legendary old pro turkey hunters, you will find that they most commonly refer to the male of the species as "gobbler" or "turkey." Take for example the first paragraph of the forward section in *The Old Pro Turkey Hunter* by Gene Nunnery.

People who read this book may have a mind that hidden in its pages may be a magic formula for killing a wild turkey. While it is probably true that any turkey hunter, young or old, will be a better turkey hunter after reading it, it could also be true, that even if the reader will learn to be a better turkey hunter, he may, in fact, actually kill fewer turkeys. How can this be? The fact is the old pro turkey hunters who march through the pages of this book are going to convince you that real turkey hunting doesn't always necessarily have to include a pile of feathers and blood. These old master turkey hunters hunted wild turkeys without having to abide by the hunting seasons, bag limits, game wardens, or any other restrictions. They found that the real reward for successful turkey hunting lay in within the battle, not necessarily exterminating the foe.

Not once did he refer to turkeys or turkey hunting in any other way than using the term "turkey." Obviously the word "turkey" could mean either a hen or gobbler, for both are turkeys, but if someone is talking about a female turkey, then they most always make use of the term "hen." Last time I checked, the state of Alabama had a Fall and Spring turkey season, and not gobbler season, even though they only allow us to shoot gobblers. Though I have absolutely no objection to the word "gobbler", the injection of northern accents into the word such that we commonly hear "gabbler this" and "gabbler that", "gabbler chasing" and "gabbler guns" on the television hunting shows has become an ear sore to me.

But if I may be allowed only one request, it would be that we throw the word "bird" out of our modern turkey hunting vocabulary. Every hunter you talk to, or hunting show host you watch, or hunting story you read now calls turkeys "birds." While it is certainly true that turkeys are birds, they hardly act like birds, and you hardly ever shoot them on the wing like birds. Besides, "bird" traditionally refers to quail, and so I try to restrict its use for matters dealing with quail hunting.

And the turkey hunting paraphernalia you see on the market today is utterly ridiculous. I once saw for sale, hanging in my nearest hunting store, a bottle of turkey scent. For those of you who have not been properly taught the difference between turkey hunting and deer hunting, let me help you a little. You do not hunt turkeys with rifles, but with shotguns loaded with shot sizes between # 2's and # 7 1/2's. You do not hunt turkeys by sitting next to green fields either. You can, but you should not. And you do not hunt turkeys with a piece of cloth soaked in turkey scent dragging behind your boot as you walk through the woods - not because you should not, but because turkey's cannot smell, at least to any appreciable extent. I thank God too. If they could, we certainly would not ever kill any.

But I must confess, I have allowed my self to be sucked into buying a few of these useless products, and after they in fact proved useless, I was quite ashamed of what I had done. Fighting calls for instance. According to the tapes I watched when they hit the market, they seemed to be the deadliest addition to turkey hunting since the invention of the shotgun. I bought them, used them, and regret the whole affair. I should have learned my lesson from an experience I once had with my father.

When I was a boy, my father always took me to the annual boat show held at the Birmingham Jefferson Civic Center. It was a good time, even though we possessed no more interest in boats than elk hunting. But, there were enough fishing booths and a few hunting booths scattered about to keep our interest for a few hours.

One night, on our way out of the show, we passed a booth that grabbed both our attentions. Perched high behind a table stood a man whose voice should have been good enough to win him a date with any woman he wished. Scattered about the white cloth table were boxes of all kinds of knives, mostly for the kitchen, and a few other queer gadgets. It was apparent that he had just started a demonstration and was attempting to sell his merchandise to those of us gathered around.

He proceeded to pull out knives and rave about how wonderfully sharp and useful they were. My father stood next to me with his arm around my shoulder and said in his deep, authoritative voice, "Watch, Son, and see foolish some people are with their money and buy things they don't need." It is important that you understand the word tight is a gross understatement of the frugality with which my father deals with money. He was a banker and very thrifty with his money. He was more than capable of discerning between the need for buying something important for his family and passing up enticing scams, and so he figured this was a good opportunity to teach me to do the same.

So there we stood and watched, and the man began to cut bread and oranges and tomatoes and even a steel pipe. If there was ever anything in this world difficult to cut, he proved his knives were more than capable for the task—plastic, carrots, steak,...Our eyes began to get a little wider. Then the man took out his gadgets and began to twist and twirl potatoes into artwork that should have gone to the local museum, but could end up on our dinner plates as french fries instead. In half a second, he turned an orange fruit into a squeeze container full of delicious pure orange juice that was fun to drink and healthy too. Now both our eyes were bulging out as our mouths hung wide open. Then the man said we could have everything, all the knives and all the gadgets, for just twenty-five dollars. But we had enough sense and resisted this temptation. We hung strong right up to the point when he offered to the first five customers the whole set for the super low special of twenty dollars. Suddenly, sliced steel pipe coming forth from the fryer seemed awfully delicious. It was not two seconds before my father handed me a twenty, and I was first in line.

That was fifteen years ago, and to date, I do not think our family has ever used these knives or gadgets to cut bread or carrots, or even to twirl potatoes into art fries, and I am absolutely positive we have never eaten sliced, fried steel pipe. I still have all my teeth. That proves it.

ABOUT THE AUTHOR

Bob Henderson, Jr. is a native of Birmingham, Alabama and is currently completing his residency in dermatology at Wake Forest University School of Medicine in North Carolina. He has spent countless days turkey hunting the central and southern counties of Alabama for over twenty years; in fact first joining his father in the turkey woods at the age of four. Next year, he plans to return to Alabama and resume hunting turkeys on a less restrictive schedule.